MAKING OUR WAY TO SHORE

A Celebration of Hebrew Baby Naming and Baptism

D0916230

By

Eileen O'Farrell Smith

"Making our Way to Shore," by Eileen O'Farrell Smith. ISBN 1-58939-549-2.

Published 2004 by Virtualbookworm.com Publishing Inc., P.O. Box 9949, College Station, TX 77845, US. ©2004, Eileen O'Farrell Smith. All rights reserved. No part of this publication may be reproduced, stored in a retrieval system, or transmitted in any form or by any means, electronic, mechanical, recording or otherwise, without the prior written permission of Eileen O'Farrell Smith.

Manufactured in the United States of America.

Amen

Be careful of simple words said often.

"Amen" makes demands
like an unrelenting schoolmaster:
fierce attention paid to all that is said;
no apathy, no preoccupation, no prejudice permitted.
"Amen": We are present. We are open.
We are of one mind. We understand.
Here we are; we are listening to your word.

"Amen" makes demands
like a signature on a dotted line:
sober bond to all that goes before;
no hesitation, no half-heartedness,
no mental reservations allowed.
"Amen": We support. We approve.
We are of one mind. We promise.
May this come to pass. So be it.

Be careful when you say "Amen".

-Barbara Schmich Searle

Dedication

To My Husband Stephen
And to our beloved children Nora, Bennett and Liliana
In whom I see the face of God

Table Of Contents

Preface

I have not always been interested in the topic of intermarriage. Growing up in the 1950's in a household of first generation Irish Catholics, the subject never entered my mind. While it was probably true that my childhood neighborhood on Long Island was predominantly Christian at the time, there were a goodly number of Jewish families so as to warrant the building of a new temple while I was in grade school. I never set foot inside this synagogue, which stood high on a nearby hill, the edifice an imposing sight to a small child. While the building appeared formidable due to its sheer height and breadth, its presence was more of mystery to me. However, I would delight as I celebrated a free day from school, as friends walked to temple to participate in rituals and holidays alien to me. They would remain foreign to me for the next twenty-five years. At that time, I never would have believed that those same rituals and Holy Days would become as familiar and cherished by me as an adult as my middle name.

The ultimate goal is to respond to each family and to help them discover a ritual that is authentic to their own vision of faith and life.

By the mid-eighties, I had married a Jewish man and we had begun our family. The concerns (primarily) of the Jewish community regarding interfaith marriage and the children of those marriages were beginning to grab my attention. All of a sudden, the newspaper stories, magazine articles and the "sound bites" became relevant, as they were talking about *my* family. Not only were they talking about myself, my husband and our three young children, but our larger 'family' of those parents and children at the Jewish Catholic Couples Dialogue Group in Chicago.

The Dialogue Group was born in the spring of 1988, as an outgrowth of Catholic-Jewish couples wanting a forum to learn and grow and teach one another. Thirteen years later, the Dialogue Group is still a unique organization: run by couples for couples and families, its mission is one of service to Catholic-Jewish couples and their families with the support of clergy (there are two Catholic priests and two Reform Rabbis who serve as 'chaplains' to the group). Monthly meetings are held throughout the year, each one serving a particular focus: informational/educational (e.g. presented in lecture format), practical (e.g. a wedding workshop) and social/spiritual (e.g. an annual Seder). One of the tenets of the founding families was the understanding that there would not be an agenda for conversion: the group's sole intent was one of support.

Since 1991, members of the Dialogue Group and our clergy have created and celebrated initiation ceremonies to welcome children into our shared faith traditions, with both a Priest and a Rabbi as co-presiders. Initially, they did so in response to the needs of the couples they had previously married, who now asked them to bless their newborn children. In the spirit of finding new pathways for interfaith families to share their traditions, they have celebrated the spiritual initiation of children into our faith communities while creating opportunities to ask deeper questions about a family's religious life in an atmosphere of open dialogue. The ultimate goal is to respond to each family and to help them discover a ritual that is  authentic to their own vision of faith and life. The ceremony that you will find here is the evolution of many years of conversation and learning between these seekers and pioneers: our clergy and these parents of the Dialogue Group.

I would like to thank the Catholic Jewish community of Chicago, and in particular the families of the Dialogue Group and the Family School, for their inspiration. For those religious scholars who took me under their wing, in particular Dr. Egon Mayer, of Blessed Memory, and Rev. John Westerhoff, I am humbly grateful for your attention and interest. I am grateful for the unconditional support of our clergy, in particular Rabbi Allen Secher formerly of Congregation Makom Shalom; Rabbi Misha Tillman; and Rabbi Michael Sternfield of Chicago Sinai Congregation for their time and talent and plentiful embrace of our family, and to Father Bernie Pietrzak, Pastor of St. Raymond de Penafort, for his guidance and support of this ministry. To the clergy of Old St. Patrick's I am particularly indebted, to Father Jack Wall the Pastor, whose original vision of mission embodies the spirit of that which we are about, and to Father John Cusick, our chaplain whose energy and enthusiasm continues to challenge and engage us, always with the underpinnings of acceptance, generosity and love. I am grateful to Jennifer Woyan for her handholding and computer savvy in formatting the original text, to Mary Holmquist for her insight regarding the cover and to Diane Chandler and her staff at the Chandler Group for their support of this ministry. To the children and artists of the Family Religion School, I am grateful for your talent and honored for the opportunity to have known you. Most importantly, I am indebted to the ACTA Foundation and its Board of Directors for their vision, generosity and support in underwriting this manuscript.

I hope this text is useful to you as a resource in your own adult faith formation, and to that of your children. As I continue to parent my children with attention to their faith lives, I have found the following words of Rabbi David Wolpe to be reassuring and wise and of great comfort in times of doubt or distress. I offer them to you now, as you go on your way:

> *"Finding our own way to faith is the best possible beginning to helping children...the key is not to take your own faith and transplant it into the soul of a child. The key is to take what you have ---your own faith, questions, ideas, even doubts---and use them to enable the child to develop his or her own way..."*

> David Wolpe, *Teaching Your Children About God*
> (New York: Henry Holt & Co., 1993)

And so, on your mark, get set, Go.....!

My Story

One of the more dominant "religious" memories of my youth concerned a request from a best friend. It was the summer of 1969 and I was eighteen. America was at war with Vietnam, and John Paul XXIII was sitting at the Vatican. I was enjoying the end of my childhood, growing up in a sleepy village on then-rural Long Island, at the time a Catholic enclave. Born into a first generation Irish Catholic family as familiar with saying the Rosary as dancing a reel, I delighted in my family's brogue, while wrestling with my mother about the appropriate length of my green plaid uniform skirt. Though I had spent my primary years at the local public school, attending the mandatory CCD program (Confraternity of Christian Doctrine) on Saturday mornings, I had transferred to Our Lady of Mercy Academy at seventh grade where I graduated six years later. My private world was bright and happy, generous and sweet and very, very uncomplicated. My best friend, a Polish girl as Catholic as I, was getting married that summer to a lovely Protestant man she had known for some time. And with a request that would stand neighborhood friends apart for life, she asked me to come to her wedding. In fact, she asked me *be in her wedding!* It was my first encounter with the strict rules of the church regarding intermarriage, as I learned I was not permitted to participate. In fact, I did not even attend. This was to be the beginning of my relationship with the interfaith world, one that has been sometimes painful, exhausting and frustrating, but always faith-filled, joyful and life-giving.

Although I had a catalogue of sins from which to choose, I often found it difficult to keep from repeating what I had said the week before, sometimes varying the *number* of infractions I had waged.

What kind of Catholic child was I? My earliest recollections of God have everything to do with religion and ritual. For example, I can remember being dragged off to confession on Saturday afternoons during the summers of my youth. I hated it on a number of levels: first we, that is my older brother and I, had to stop what we were doing and get ready to go. This often entailed a vigorous 'clean up', as you couldn't go to church looking like you had just been dragged out of the pool, which is where we had usually come from. Although I had a catalogue of sins from which to choose, I often found it difficult to keep from repeating what I had said the week before, sometimes varying the *number* of infractions I had waged. As best as I can remember now, those numbers were always arbitrary, rarely an accurate reflection of the week's past behavior. During these early years I don't think I ever thought of God as scary or threatening, save for the depictions I knew to be in my parent's copy of *Dante's Inferno*, with illustrations by Gustav Dore, which detailed horrific pictures of hell and purgatory. In fact, my experience of life was one of loving, kindness and acceptance found at home, which I am sure I projected onto the Almighty. With infantile belief, I recall personalizing God, floating somewhere in the sky looking down on me at all times.

Our religious family life was one of a typical devout Catholic family in the 1950's. My parents, who had known *each other's parents* before they themselves had met, were steadfast and loyal to their faith traditions and the role those traditions would play in their family as it grew. I celebrated all the Sacraments at the appropriate times: baptism at one month, communion at seven and confirmation in the spring of 8th grade. My only vivid, and some might argue most profound, recollection of any of these proceedings came during the reception of First Eucharist. As the tallest girl in my class, I was the last to process to the altar. Upon receiving Communion I returned to my pew only to vomit what was left of the Lord's body, now clinging to my upper

palette. The good Sisters of Mercy, however, marched me back to the altar to receive again. To this day I am tempted to weep at the reminiscence of the shame, humiliation and self-contempt I felt then.

As a matter of course, our family went to weekly Sunday Mass as well as Mass on every Holy Day of Obligation; ashes were received on Ash Wednesday, and a proper penance created and observed throughout the course of Lent (as well as the traditional Friday Lenten dinner of fish and spaghetti); and a crucifix and other religious icons were displayed in prominent positions in our house--most notably a large statue of Mary crushing an asp with her foot, taking center stage resting in the hallway alcove. Praying was ever-present in the family: grace was said at dinnertime, and nighttime prayers were offered on one's knees. I have a vivid recollection of having a scapula hanging from my neck in the earlier part of my youth, though I remember more of what it felt like to have plastic digging into my skin than its significance. Apart from our family rituals, my parents were instrumental in the formation of a new parish, directing the men's and women's councils, Pre-Cana and teaching CCD. Religion in its entire splendor bound me to the faith of my forefathers.

And so it continued through my college years and beyond. I attended a Catholic university and chose a career in medicine, motivated in large measure by my keen sense of wanting to serve my fellow man. Not accepted to *any* medical school immediately after college and having been molded by a very strong sense of Catholic social justice, I joined first the Peace Corps working in Zaire teaching science in French, and then VISTA, where I taught reading to young adults who had been passed through the educational system in spite of failing. Though most Peace Corpsman will admit to a desire to see the world and travel a bit while doing some good, I can assure you that was not my case. I was driven by what had been indoctrinated years earlier, the call by Jesus to help those less fortunate. The way I chose to live my life was based on the belief that I did so because it was mandated by God.

Flash forward to the mid-1970's. Through a mutual friend at work, I met my future husband Stephen, a Boston Jew. I had never dated anyone from another religion before, nor in fact did I, as an adult, know many Jewish people. Now in my mid-thirties, dating someone living within the framework of a different faith tradition never entered my mind as a cause for concern or hesitation. I loved and respected him, as he did me. We accepted each other the way we were. We were best friends, and it soon became obvious that we would marry.

I remember this as a time of pain and regret, for my intention had never been to be a 'do nothing' family, which is what we had become.

But what would we do about the children, should they arrive? I can remember a few conversations we had, usually late at night and always ending with no resolution. I think neither one of us wanted to "give up" our own position. He felt the children would figure it out on their own as they grew; I felt with a little persistence, I would wind up getting my way, for after all, I was the "devoted" one! Rather than fight about it, we just let it go, knowing that in our love for one another, we would find a way to make it work. How naïve we were!

Within the first five years of our marriage, we were blessed with three children. By the time our oldest daughter was five, Steve was still content with the path of least resistance--that being "we'll let the children figure it out for themselves." He had felt confident enough to express a concern that should I and the children "be Catholic", he would feel left out, an experience that left him feeling scared, inadequate and best left unexplored. I, on the other hand, was in a constant state of anxiety over what I wasn't doing for my children. With feelings bordering on desperation every time a friend had a child baptized, I longed for some clarity and action (and surely some repetition of what I had so lovingly experienced as a child). At that time, we had no vision of what we were about as a family. Though I was still singing in the church choir and attending weekly Mass, I would go alone, this time now being relegated to "dad's time" with the children. We had not joined a church together, or a temple. I remember this as a time of pain and regret, for my intention had never been to be a 'do-nothing' family, which is what we had become.

What happened next could best be described as a conversionary experience, for all involved. I noticed an article during the Easter/Passover season in *The Chicago Tribune*, regarding a couples-led group ministered to by both a priest and a rabbi. Steve was willing to make the call to the priest, Father John Cusick of Old St. Pat's and the Archdiocesan Office of Young Adult Ministry. This initial call has now developed into an eleven-year-old profound relationship with the clergy, the group and our religious communities of origin. I believe this call altered the course of our family and the faith formation of ourselves, *as well as* that of our children. Through the support, encouragement and auspices of the group and its clergy, we were able to bless our children in a Hebrew Naming and Baptism ceremony in December of 1992, which in fact became the inspiration for this text. One year later, Steve and I, along with five other families, formed the Catholic Jewish Religious Family School. In the spring of 1996, again with the participation and support of our Catholic and Jewish clergy, our two older children celebrated their First Eucharist, soon followed by their younger sibling.

Over the years, our family has evolved into a Catholic Jewish family, made manifest in a variety of ways. We celebrate with delight and joy the holidays of both of our faiths: Christmas and Easter, Passover and Hanukkah, Lent and Advent, Purim and Sukkot. We say grace at the dinner table in the shadow of a cross and a mezuzah, one placed under the other on our doorpost. We display our Nativity set alongside our collection of menorahs, spinning dreidels adjacent to our advent calendar, while performing daily acts of kindness to one another on the countdown towards Christmas. I will get ashes on Ash Wednesday, Steve will fast on Yom Kippur, each with the respect, support and understanding of our partner. We have joined a church, Old St. Patrick's, where both Steve and I are active. Steve sits on a number of committees, while I sing in the church choir. We have joined a reform Jewish congregation, Chicago Sinai, with both of us contributing our time and talent in a community where we are embraced as a family. Our children have become as fluent in the recitation of the *Our Father* as they are in reciting the Hebrew brakhas (or blessings) for Shabbat. In the past eight years, we have as a family attended Rosh Hoshana services, as well as those on Yom Kippur (including one date which fell on our son's eighth birthday!). We rarely, if ever, miss the 11:15 Sunday morning mass, often joking that someone is sitting in our pew if we arrive later than usual! A number of years ago, we joined the local Museum of Judaica (Spertus Institute) as a family, where we avail ourselves of the many wondrous offerings they have for families, from making Seder plates to going on an archeological 'dig', as well as seminars, lectures and graduate level classes.

> I believe that children have an inherent faith and the circumstances of their life's journey will foster or inhibit it. The key, I believe is having children feel beloved, then enhanced by ritual, stories and worship.

And what of Jesus? I *understand* that he was a human figure, born to a Jewish family. I *believe* that he was God incarnate, that he truly was Love in human form. There is no 'party line' in the family. I have made it very clear to my children what I believe about Christ, and how he moves through my life. They understand the Jewish sense of Jesus in a significant way and they seem to be open to learning and studying and wrestling and challenging all that comes to them. It is important to remember that we have three children, all individuals with different interests and unique abilities and, most importantly, their own spirituality. I cannot assume that they will all grow and learn and believe the same things at the same time. One can't forget how grace and mystery moves through their lives.

And what of my own journey of faith? I would have to say that my beliefs are still evolving. I think of God as a power, an essence that creates all, no longer a bearded figure in the sky. I think of God as love; this love is the power by which all things happen. In teaching our children I emphasize the aspect of God as the Creator of all; the concept of the Godliness in each of us; the importance of God's gifts to us in the form of rules and laws; and to stress and stress again God's intimate love of them. Being Catholic is important to me: I am Catholic, and it is woven into my very being, like my shadow. Yet the strength and vitality of my Catholicism comes not from Rome and the 'formal' church: it is the personal, transforming aspect of being a Catholic that  compels me. Years ago I would have stated how critically important it was to me that my children be Catholic when they are adults, usually with the accompanying feelings of guilt, panic and distress should they choose otherwise. While I have found great comfort, strength, delight and faith from my religious tradition, I have come to know there are other true paths to God. I believe that children have an inherent faith, and the circumstances of their life's journey will foster or inhibit it. The key, I believe, is having children feel beloved, then enhancing their lives with ritual, stories and worship. By our actions, our children will find their way. Steve and I have been committed to these actions because we have an adult appreciation of faith and ritual and God in our lives, and by doing what we do, we show them our vision, the path to a relationship with the Almighty One. In addition, Steve and I do everything together and we do it with ease, naturally, and with joy. A friend asked me not long ago how it was to be involved in two different religious traditions. While owning up to constant fatigue, I said something like "we don't do soccer, we do church", which in hindsight is profoundly true. We make it a priority to attend worship services, both Catholic and Jewish, above all other activities. Whether it's Friday evening or Sunday morning, that's what comes first.

Ultimately, what is important is that our children love God and love one another: that they come to recognize the divine in themselves, and in each other.

And so, I have come full circle in my relationship with intermarriage: from a refusal to participate in my best friend's wedding, to helping my daughter negotiate Hebrew verbs thirty years later. In the interim, while becoming closer to my own God, I have embraced a partner, respecting his traditions and faith, and in so doing have experienced the love of one true God, the God we share.

Intermarriage, Children, and the Question of Faith

Before we move to an understanding of the rites of initiation and their meaning within the interfaith family, it is of value to stop for a moment and review the status of intermarriage in general. For whether it's being written about on the front page of the New York Times, or being discussed at the board meetings of one's local Temple, the question of intermarriage is one posing grave concern to the American Jewish population. A 1990 study by the Council of Jewish Federations found that the proportion of Jews marrying outside their community is 52 percent[1] (as opposed to 21 percent for the Catholic community, 30 percent for the Mormons and 40 percent for Muslims, as identified in a 1990 survey by author/psychologist Joel Crohn, Ph.D. [2]), thus posing a threat to the very future of the Jewish population in this country. In addition, as a percentage of the general population, the number of Jews has fallen from about 4 percent to a little over 2 percent. In the words of Steven Bayme, National Director of Communal Affairs at the American Jewish Committee as quoted in New York magazine:

> "The numbers are of serious concern. The real impact of the intermarriage numbers hasn't been felt yet. If someone married in the last couple of years, we don't know how those children will be raised....it's possible we could go down from 5 and a half million people (where we are now) to 4 million over the next twenty years. In the shadow of having lost one third of our population in the Holocaust, losing people through cultural assimilation is demoralizing. A society losing numbers is a society of decadence." [3]

And a society of diminished numbers translates to a society of diminished intellectual, political, economical and cultural riches, he infers.

Whereas one hundred years ago, a marriage partner might have been chosen based on ethnic background, parental introduction and/or acceptance or familiar values, today's couples will probably marry for love, so the social scientists will have us believe. The Jewish Outreach Institute, based in New York City, concludes that while those numbers for intermarriage are high, they are a "by-product of other large scale transformations in American family life affecting Jews and non-Jews alike."[4] These alterations include "the removal of social barriers between Jews and non-Jews in work, education and in their leisure activities; the later age of marriage; a geographic shift away from older areas of dense Jewish concentrations; increased participation of women in the work force; and the increased incidence of divorce and remarriage."[5]

Dr. Egon Mayer, Sociologist and America's leading student of interfaith marriage and former director of the JOI, points out four categories of marriage when Jews and Christians intermarry. In his book *Love and Tradition: Marriage Between Jews and Christians*[6], he identifies the first as a conversionist marriage (about 33% of intermarriages) whereby the Christian partner converts to Judaism. The second, so states Dr. Mayer, is the assimilationist marriage (approx. 10%) where the Jewish partner converts to Christianity. The third type of marriage is the largest, representing 43% of intermarriages, where neither spouse converts and they go about sharing and blending their traditions into a culture of their own making. The remaining percent (15%) are those families who reject all links and commitments to their traditions, and forego being identified with a group.

In support of Dr. Mayer's conclusions, an additional perspective is offered regarding a family's psychodynamic emotional development. According to Dr. Joel Crohn in his above mentioned book *Mixed Matches*, families usually accommodate themselves to one of five paths when confronted with interethnic, interfaith differences. Simply stated, they are: first, the *universalistic* path, whereby couples create an identity new to each of them, taking bits and pieces of their past and aligning them in a new way; second, the *minimalistic* path, where families are secular in manner, taking little or nothing from their past and become a unit unto itself rather than have a stake in a larger community; third, the *balanced solution*, where couples work to includes aspects of both traditions, balancing the importance of each; fourth, *two cultures, one religion*, where one member of the family converts or actively participates in the religion of the other without conversion, recognizing their different cultural roots while celebrating one religion; and finally, *one culture, one religion*, where couples immerse themselves into one culture and one religion, with one partner totally assimilating themselves into the operational community (pg.150).[7]

According to the National Jewish Population Survey, **in 1990** there were at least 770,000 children of Jewish intermarriage under the age of 18.[8] To begin to understand the issues regarding the children of intermarried parents, one has to revisit the literature beginning with that from the 1930's. In 1937, Sociologist Everett Stonequist presented his concept of the "marginal man" after studying the intermarried populations of Hawaii, India and England. While these children may have a broader vision of different cultures and may experience a greater mobility between these heritages, he found that ultimately they suffer: at home with both, they belonged to neither. He stated:

> "The individual who is unwillingly initiated into two or more historic traditions, languages, political loyalties, moral codes or religions is a marginal man....who will experience the conflict as an acute personal difficulty or mental tension...having a double consciousness, it is as if he were placed simultaneously between two looking-glasses, each presenting a sharply different image of himself. The clash in the images gives rise to a mental conflict as well as to a dual self-consciousness and identification..."[9]

In addition, he found these "marginals" to find non-acceptance and intolerance from their two originating communities, and to have feelings of inferiority, ambiguity, hypersensitivity, irritability, moodiness and feelings of emotional ambivalence!

A later survey concluded in 1957 by James Bossard and Eleanor Stoker Boll also studied the social and emotional status of children from interfaith marriages. Using data collected from family case histories over a period of twenty-five years, they interwove information from children, parents, relatives and grandparents. As depicted in their book *One Marriage, Two Faiths*, they sought to study whether or not children of intermarriages would develop neurosis as a result of the conflict of having to choose between two religious paths, or more pointedly, two religious "truths" of their parents. They detailed a number of patterns within a family regarding how these issues were managed, including how the more dominant parent "took over"; how religious identification was prearranged into certain categories, such as the girls will be one thing, the boys will be another; a "hands off" policy where children were left to decide for themselves; and a complete lack of conviction to do anything, eliciting continual family conflict. In terms of religious identity, the researchers found that the children ultimately decided for themselves their own identity **regardless** of what their parent had decided. They concluded:

> "...it has been pointed out that people who make interfaith marriages apparently will realize that children will cause problems or will have problems. The lower birth rate and higher rate of childlessness among such couples suggest this. A part of this difficulty is caused by a primary function of the family ---to pass down the cultural heritage. When the parents are of different religions, the family is a cultural mixture and the child is torn, in choosing his religion and his philosophy of life, between two sides of the family. This results not only in 'taking sides' within the family, but in inner conflict for the child. This divisiveness extends to brothers and sisters as well as to parents, and tends to separate them even when they grow up, marry and have their own children who are reared in various faiths."[10]

At about the same time, in a now-famous study, Harvard student Philip Rosten wrote an undergraduate honors thesis detailing the lives of 15 Harvard and Radcliffe students, each a child of a Jewish and a Gentile parent. He named this group the *mischlings*, a Yiddish term translated as "mixed one," and set about to study this population, searching for specific unique qualifications. Most of these individuals had a Jewish father and a Protestant mother; for the most part, the Jews were well assimilated with no religious ties to the Jewish community. Their families tended to live their lives within the Christian majority. Louis Berman, in his 1968 book *Jews and Intermarriage*, highlighted the major findings of this research: despite the lack of Jewishness in their upbringing, only 3 of the 15 *mischlings* identified themselves as Gentile. Their Jewish identification came, therefore, from "the culture-less home, Gentile unfriendliness and the allure of Jewishness."[11] While being raised in a secular environment, most of the *mischlings* were shocked to experience anti-Semitism for the first time, being unprepared for it. At the same time, their peer-group of Gentiles did not accept them and ostracized them from the group. From a peer group of Jews who welcomed them into their group, they felt accepted and a sense of belonging, creating a sense of pride in their Jewish heritage.

There were other problems that Rosten discovered. Some *mischlings* had difficulty coping with a world that wouldn't validate their own Gentile self-image. Others were "confused and indecisive about where their Jewishness ends and their Gentileness begins."[12]   The majority felt "they live in a limbo between the two groups, not a Jew, not a Gentile, but a unique combination of both."[13] He concluded, therefore, that these *mischlings* lacked a sense of where they belonged, feeling ethnically isolated from either community: most "constantly viewed life through a prism of two cultures."[14] From a sociological perspective, the group seemed to value their access to both communities; they used this ability as a passport, to "wander between the two groups with a unique mixture of subjective participation and objective observation."[15]

One of the most well-respected studies found in contemporary literature is the one conducted by Dr. Egon Mayer in 1983 entitled *Children of Intermarriage: A Study in Patterns of Identification and Family Life*. In research underwritten by the American Jewish Committee, he sought to understand how children of intermarrieds viewed themselves, both ethnically and religiously; to document the relationships between parents and children and children and grandparents in intermarried families; and to determine whether children born of an interfaith marriage feel insecure and as if they do not belong.

Using as a population base of 117 children, ages 16 through 46, from intermarried couples who had participated in an earlier study (entitled *Intermarriage and the Jewish Future*, published in 1976 by the American Jewish Committee), Dr. Mayer divided his participants into two groups: those from conversionary marriages (that is where the Gentile-born parent converted to Judaism) and the others from mixed marriages (where neither partner converted). Regarding the issue of identity when comparing children of mixed marriages versus children of conversionary marriages, a number of findings were noteworthy[16]:

- Most of the children of conversionary marriages considered themselves Jewish; while only one quarter of those of mixed marriages did;

- Children of conversionary marriages took great pride in being Jewish, while children of mixed marriages felt "indifferent" to it;

- Children of conversionary marriages were more likely to observe Jewish holidays, celebrate Jewish rites of passage, receive a more intense Jewish education and have more Jewish objects at home;

- Children of conversionary marriages were very similar to the American Jewish population in general regarding Jewish philanthropy: however, regarding their attitude of the religious life of the Jewish community and regarding the state of Jewish peoplehood, they were similar to those children of mixed marriage. In fact many reported observing Christmas as well as Hanukkah and some even reported observing Easter as well as Passover.

At the same time:

- Both groups felt their religious identity was more important than their ethnic heritage;
- Both groups felt a similar sense of pride related to Israel's accomplishments;
- Both groups thought of their Jewishness as a private matter;
- Both groups preferred home celebrations over attendance at synagogue, preferring to "study at home";
- Both groups stated they felt as comfortable with Jewish friends as with non-Jews; and
- Over one third of the married children from the conversionary families had a non-Jewish partner; an overwhelming majority of married children from mixed marriages had married a non-Jew.

Regarding the question of marginality, Dr. Mayer concluded:

> Children of intermarriage do not feel any keen pangs of conflict or confusion about themselves, nor do they have fractured relationships with their parents or families. Marginality and all its associated psychological perils undoubtedly plague some, but most are unperturbed by their dual heritage. The increasing incidence of intermarriage and the declining significance of ethnic and religious differences between Jews and Christians, in general, have probably lessened the emotional consequences of being raised in an intermarried home."[17]

In a more recent research document, Ph.D. candidate Juliet Whitcomb (Adelphi University, 1996) entitled her dissertation *Mixed*

Up or Just Mixed? Adjustment of Children in Interfaith Families, which sought to compare the psychological adjustment of children from non-conversionary and conversionary families to children of same-faith families. Using data drawn from the 1988 National Survey of Families and Households, the study predicted that children from same-faith marriages would be better adjusted than children from conversionary marriages, who in turn would be better adjusted than children from interfaith marriages. In particular, she hypothesized that children from interfaith marriages would experience, as reported by their parents, more unhappiness, more behavior problems, more depression and anxiety, inferior academic achievement and poorer quality of child-parent relationships than children of same-faith or conversionary marriages, as reported by *their* parents.

Dr. Whitcomb's findings were starkly different from those reported elsewhere in the literature. Contrary to expectations, there were "no significant differences" among children of same-faith, interfaith or conversionary marriages on any of the adjustment-related points, of which there were 32. She summarized:

> "The results of this study, therefore strongly contradict prior assertions in the anecdotal literature that religious differences between parents will be detrimental to children's well being...Also contrary to expectations, children from interfaith families were found to have no greater adjustment problems than children from conversionary families. Moreover, though the impact of religious child rearing strategies on adjustment was not directly assessed (in the present study), this finding suggests that children from conversionary families who are likely to have a single religious identity, and those from interfaith families who were less likely to have a single religious identification, fare equally well." [18]

Most of the aforementioned comments have been prepared for the academic community. What is available for the 'man in the pew'? A trip to the local book store or public library will undoubtedly yield a variety of books addressed to the lay population searching for information and answers on how to manage an interfaith relationship, and more specifically "what to do about the children." In *Raising Your Jewish/Christian Child,* author Lee Gruzen offers advice on how to blend both Jewish and Christian traditions into one home. Using her own interfaith family and their journey as a template, she offers advice on a variety of topics (how to deal with grandparents, talking with your children about God, celebrating holidays), always with the underpinning of coming to an understanding of both traditions with respect and awe. She states candidly that "the task of choosing a birth rite for our daughters required more formalized religious commitment on our part, more enlightenment on the part of our families, and overall, more hard work, knowledge and emotional risk  than we were prepared to muster at that time"[19], therefore choosing to do nothing. Authors Judy Petsonk and Jim Remsen in *The Intermarriage Handbook* offer a practical self-help book covering courtship and marriage through death and burial. There is also a chapter on Baptism and Jewish rites of passage, noting "a rite of passage is a very special kind of celebration. By giving you a moment elevated above the ordinary, it is supposed to help you make the transition to a new stage of life."[20] In their chapter on identity, they maintain that their research leads to the conclusion that children fare better if they are brought up in one religion, not two. Petsonk and Remsen opine that a child might be exposed to celebrations and beliefs of a second religion, but they should assume the religious identity of only one parent, for "the child raised in one religion knows who he is."[21] The book also offers an excellent overview of the history of Jewish Christian relations, beginning with the earliest Gospel writers through the creation of the Vatican's Office of Catholic Jewish Relations in 1969.

Authors Mary Helene Rosenbaum and husband Ned Rosenbaum walk couples through their thirty-six year marriage as a Catholic Jewish couple in their book *Celebrating Our Differences: Living Two Faiths in One Marriage*. While offering advice on topics such as how to marry, and to convert or not convert, the Rosenbaums center each topic by asking the question "where is God in your lives?" as one goes about each day, celebrating the interfaith lives one family is creating. They speak with great eloquence on their own experience regarding the Baptisms and Hebrew Baby Namings of their three children. The 1987 book *Mixed Blessings: Marriage Between Jews and*

Christians written by Paul and Rachel Cowan highlights interviews with 300 interfaith couples who, for the most part, are floundering in their relationships. Divided into three sections, the book first deals with the author's interfaith marriage, including Rachel's conversion to Judaism; the second section describes the role that intermarriage has played in the minds of Jews and Christians throughout American history; and lastly it offers practical advice based on their workshops and interviews. Susan Weidman Schneider in her book *Intermarriage: The Challenge of Living with Differences Between Christians and Jews* studies whether it is possible for partners of different religious traditions to build a relationship while remaining connected to their own religious identity. The author is skeptical of the current view that the blending of two traditions might be successful, and argues that attempting to raise children as "both" is rarely satisfying to either

> Unlike circumcision, which is a rite identifying a (male) child with a people, baptism is the ritual in which a person is identified with a faith, connected to a divine being. As such, it is essentially a private covenant.

children or parent. Rather, she finds that selecting one religious identity for the child, while respecting the other parent's traditions, works best in most cases (that one identity being Judaism).[22]

There are additional books in the marketplace offering families additional research and consideration, with little or no perspective on Baptism nor reference to sacramental life. The first, by psychologist Joel Crohn, while different in its orientation as it deals with issues of racial, cultural and interfaith differences, is still a solid resource. In *Mixed Matches: How to Create successful Interracial, Interethnic and Interfaith Relationships*, Dr. Crohn, using his personal experience as well as that garnered from years of working with couples and families, teaches families how to cope with the many complex issues of combining two different traditions in one family. This book provides tools to help negotiate cultural contrasts, deal with extended families, overcome social barriers and raise children with a clear sense of identity, "for differences are the source of learning and creativity in all of our important relationships and learning to recognize, appreciate and use these differences are the keys to enriching family life."[23] In *Strangers to the Tribe*, journalist and author Gabrielle Glazer highlights the pathways chosen by eleven interfaith families, painting a unique portrait of each.

Arguing against the gloom-and-doom scenario, Ms. Glazer contends that her interviews pointed out those Jews who intermarry do in fact make a serious effort to pass on to their children the identity and culture of their ancestors. Based on her research, she posits that Judaism will survive intermarriage. In the last of the three, Elliot Abrams in his new book *Faith or Fear: How Jews Can Survive in a Christian America* speaks indirectly to the issue of intermarriage, while painting broad strokes depicting the rise of the secular liberal Jewish community of current America. In so doing, he argues the only "solution" against the loss of Judaism in the 21st century is a return to a religious Judaism and "a faith in God."[24]

Two additional texts are prominent in a review of contemporary material issued by National Jewish organizations. The first, published in 1993 by the Union of American Hebrew Congregations and written by Andrea King, is entitled *If I'm Jewish and You're Christian, What are the Kids?* Written with a strong bias for raising children within the Jewish community, the author clearly believes that raising children in a dual-religion home is not a viable option. She states: "Exposing children to elements of two religions rarely gives them the sense of identity, the emotional security and the consistent moral code that a single positive religious affiliation provides." (pg. 3)[25] Ms. King writes using the perspective of two imaginary composite families: one interfaith family has chosen to raise their children Jewish, yielding children secure in themselves, well-adjusted in their identity and comfortable in their religious experiences; the other family has chosen to give their children the "best" of both religions, whereby the children appear confused, alienated and lacking in moral foundation. The second book, written by New York Conservative Rabbi Alan Silverstein and entitled *It All Begins With a Date*, examines the high rates of Jewish intermarriage and offers solutions to "cure the illness." Declaring that every Jewish adult is "at risk" of intermarrying, the author highlights ways to spread the message throughout the Jewish community to date only Jews and marry only Jews, giving Jewish parents and grandparents some tools to "say no" to their children regarding intermarriage.[26]

* * *

And what of the faith of these children? All of the above has elucidated clearly the need to give children a sense of belonging and a sense of identity, whether within one community or two. But what about religious faith? What is faith? Is that also a parent's responsibility, something a parent can demand of a child? Where do we begin to unravel what one means by the word *faith* and its development in the lives of our children? Certainly, one cannot have a conversation about Baptism without serious consideration of faith.

For purposes of clarity and semantics, it is important to understand what is meant by certain words--words which are often used interchangeably, but which can mean very different things: **religion, belief** and **faith**. In his book *Faith Development in the Adult Life Cycle*, author Ken Stokes provides a good overview of the meaning of each of these words. Dr. Stokes writes:

> *"**Religion** refers to the cumulative traditions of the faith of a people in history. It includes the wide variety of sacred writings, symbols, liturgical expressions, creeds, artistic expressions, ethical teachings, etc., that make up the **religion** of a given group or individual within that group. It is a relatively stable and formalized structure of relationships which bind people together in a common purpose. **Faith** is much deeper and more personal than religion. It is part of the inner dynamic of an individual and/or that unstructured and often verbally inexpressible bond of commonality in dealing with life's ultimate issues which may be shared by two or more individuals. **Faith** necessitates a fundamental alignment of the heart and will, a commitment of loyalty and trust. **Beliefs** are ways by which faith expresses itself. They are the expressions of the human's need to communicate and to translate experiences into concepts or propositions. **Beliefs** usually take the form of words, sentences, statements, doctrines and creeds by which they, of necessity, become something outside the individual which the person can only intellectually affirm, deny or question."*[27]

Armed with a minute understanding of the vocabulary, one should also have an elementary knowledge of 'developmental' theory; while it may not be necessary to be fluent in these matters, having a sense of the lexicon gives the non-specialist a degree of reassurance in an otherwise daunting milieu. One of the first formulations of developmental theory is credited to Danish-born psychoanalyst Erik

Erickson, born at the turn of the century. His theory of development stated that personality evolves in eight stages, from early infancy to late adulthood. At each stage, the person faces a task which results from the interaction of biological, cultural and psychological influences. The person's adaptation to the task results in a crisis of sorts, in the form of a conflict between alternative attitudes. The tension involved in the conflict is eventually resolved in a favorable or unfavorable manner (for example, during the period of late infancy, the 'toddler' will struggle between the favorable attitude of autonomy versus the unfavorable attitude of shame and doubt). Erickson believed that each stage is related to the other, that each attitude exists in some form from birth till death and that the overall health of the personality is determined by whether the crises are resolved successfully or not.[28]

It cannot be overstated that the faith life of a child is but a journey and constantly changing.

At about the same time, psychologist Jean Piaget and his colleagues in Switzerland were also formulating developmental theories about how children think and express themselves. Piaget's research demonstrated that human beings develop their mental processes in a series of four different stages (he defined a 'stage' as a set of mental operations used by a person in thinking about something in particular).[29] While his work centered primarily on the way a person thinks and reasons about physical reality (that is, space, time, casual relations, weight, speed and all of that), he also investigated a child's use of language and symbol in play, the child's way of accounting for the origins of the visible universe and the child's development of moral judgment. It is interesting to note, while some of his early writings were of a religious nature, he never sought to study children's thinking about religion. (Lawrence Kohlberg was greatly influenced by the work of Piaget and his studies of moral development have extended the theories of Piaget. For the past thirty years, Kohlberg has dominated the field of research, creating a sequence of six stages that describe the methods of reasoning and judgment that people use in making moral decisions.[30])

Soon to enter the discussion was a young Methodist minister named James Fowler, conducting workshops on faith, counseling people and listening. During the course of his work, he began to see patterns emerge from the stories people were telling. Immersed in the works of

Eric Erickson and others, Dr. Fowler moved to the Harvard Divinity School, where he taught his students the beginnings of his formulations on the 'stages' of faith: that there were discernable phases that begin in childhood and on through adulthood that shape the journey of one's faith.

Building on the works of Piaget and working in close relationship with Lawrence Kohlberg (also at Harvard at this time), James Fowler's research led to a structural approach to faith development. While one can be overwhelmed by the complexity of his language, the chart below highlights, in simple laymen's terms, an orientation to his findings:

STAGE ONE: INTUITIVE-PROJECTIVE FAITH (ages 4-7)

- Have a hard time seeing things from, or understanding another's point of view,
- Do what is right to avoid punishment,
- Family is understood to mean "immediate" family,
- Learning happens primarily by observing and identifying role models, by acting and reacting, testing, touching and experiencing the world,
- God can be trusted,
- Can remember random segments of stories but can't always separate fact from fantasy.

STAGE TWO: MYTHIC-LITERAL FAITH (ages 7-12)

- Able to take on the role of the group but cannot yet see things or understand through their own eyes,
- Do what is right when it is in best interests,
- Family is understood to refer to "those like us" (in familial, ethnic, racial, class and religious terms),
- Their role models are those that validate the norms and sanctions,
- Stories and trusted authority figures are important to the understanding of "how things are", because they lack the ability to reflect on the spiritual meanings of the stories,
- Symbols, like stories, have one-dimensional literal meanings.

STAGE THREE: SYNTHETIC-CONVENTIONAL FAITH (adolescent 12-18 and/or adult 18+)

- Aware of shared feelings, agreements and expectations which take precedence over individual interests,
- Do what is right in the eyes of others in order to be seen as a good person in their eyes,
- Look for identity from others,
- Family is understood to refer to the group(s) to which one belongs and with whom one has relationships,
- Can articulate what has been taught, but not what it means or why one believes it,
- Symbols, such as the Star of David or cross, are important for how they make one feel.

STAGE FOUR: INDIVIDUATIVE-REFLECTIVE FAITH (ages 18+)

- Can engage in objective reflection and think critically about what one believes and why, then take a position on one's own to establish a personal identity,
- Takes the point of view of a system that defines rules and roles,
- Doing what is right is important to avoid a breakdown of the system,
- Consideration is given to one's place within the system in order to maintain it,
- Family is understood to refer to "those who think and act" in accordance with rules and norms one has selected for oneself,
- Symbols are reduced to the meanings or ideas they suggest,
- Authority and norms must be congruent with self-selected perspectives.

STAGE FIVE: PARADOXICAL-CONJUNCTIVE FAITH (ages 35+)

- Can compare, contrast and engage in critical reflection on what we believe in relation to what others believe,
- Open to new ways of looking at things and to seeing other viewpoints without necessarily judging them,
- The rights of the individual take precedence over the rules, that is sometimes the rules have to be disobeyed to protect the individual,

- Doing what is right means taking care of the rights of all people, even those in the minority,
- Family is understood to refer to all human beings, therefore one is vulnerable to the "truth" or "claims" of other groups or traditions,
- Authority is based on a dialectical joining of our learnings and experiences with the learnings and experiences of others,
- Symbols have the power to evoke feelings and ideas and point beyond themselves.

STAGE SIX: UNIVERSALIZING FAITH (ages 50+)

- One looks at life through the eyes of universal principles to which they are committed,
- One acts on the commitments they have made, even at great personal risk,
- Family is understood to refer to the whole human family of mankind.

---adapted from a conversation with Dr. L. Richard Bradley[31]

Another contribution to the understanding of the dynamics of faith comes from author V. Bailey Gillespie. Thinking the work of James Fowler to be insightful to theorists but of limited use to those searching for application within a pastoral setting, or for those involved in religious education, he set about to construct his own understanding of faith as experienced throughout the life cycle. His models of faith then are not stages, but rather *situations*, the ways in which one senses God in their lives. By understanding these situations of faith, he postulates, one can nurture the faith experience as one grows. Paraphrasing Dr. Gillespie from his book "The Experience of Faith" (Religious Education Press, 1988), an overview of his seven faith situations is as follows:

Situation One: Borrowed Faith (early childhood). This first expression of faith is seen in the lives and actions of others significant to a child. The child 'borrows'[32] the faith experience which is owned by someone else. Basic trust is established within the safe, nurturing, loving environment at home through the parents or parental figures. This situation teaches

God's trustworthiness. As the ages of 5 and 6 approach, a different emphasis occurs, as seen below.

Situation Two: Reflected Faith (middle childhood, ages 7-12). The child realizes he is a member of a community. In the past, it was to the faith of the family the child looked; now it is to others in the community the child looks. The young child finds God as one who is caring and loving, much like the group itself. Feelings of belonging and acceptance are the basic religious experience during this time. Faith is not just someone else's faith now, as it becomes mirrored in the life of the child. It is at this time the child delights in learning the stories and images of the community, with heroes and heroines important as "faith guarantors."[33]

Situation Three: Personalized Faith (early adolescence, 13-16). Some of the qualities found in this situation are searching, questioning and examining one's life. This is a time of critical thinking, where reflecting, refining and rejecting can occur. Faith is now becoming owned by the youth. This is a period of personal upheaval and reorganization, where faith is beginning to be very personal. According to Dr. Gillespie "this new faith is personal faith and is beginning to be found in the situations of sorting and examining...theological functioning is beginning and abstract thinking is a reality in their lives.[34]"

Situation Four: Interior or Established Faith (later youth 15-18). This fourth situation comes after the time of questioning and sorting. Established faith means having an identity in God. 'Knowing' is important, for if one is going to own something, one should know what it is. For the time being, beliefs have been solidified and now take a back seat to other life concerns.

Situation Five: Reordered Faith (young adult, 18-28). This fifth form reinterprets personal faith. At this time, the questioning and searching for identity is past and faith now is more focused, yielding to a more introspective testing. Remythologizing has begun to take place where new meanings are given to old structures and old information. Career, marriage, jobs, children and God all seem to be happening at the same time. One tests basic faith structures in the practical world.

Situation Six: Reflective Faith (middle adult). Life is now seen in a very broad perspective, reducing life to the basics, of "God and future, integrity and hopefulness."[35] There is now a sense of urgency that is experienced both in the social and religious area: an awareness that time is of the essence to succeed and to make one's mark. The experience of God now brings a sense of confidence and security. During this time, there is a renewed interest in devotional and spiritual growth (hence the crowded retreat centers and spirituality sections in bookstores, so suggests Dr. Gillespie!).

Situation Seven: Resolute Faith (older adult). Decisions made earlier in life now settle in comfortably. One characteristic of resolute faith is wisdom. It is also a time for making sense out of things that happen. In addition, in the face of uncertainty, with the prospect of poor health and the death of friends, this is a time of deep reflection, potential anxiety and solitude. God is seen as the comforter. One remembers the actions of God and begins to make sense of reality and find hope in the future.

Acknowledging the stages 'synthetic-conventional', 'individuative-reflexive' and the remaining others and with a bow of gratitude to his friend James Fowler, theologian John Westerhoff III made an additional contribution, within a pastoral framework, of his own. Acknowledging that faith is a "verb, that is a way of behaving and in action among others"[36], Rev. Westerhoff has offered yet another way of looking at the development of faith through the suggestion of 'styles' of faith in his book *Will Our Children Have Faith?*, of which there are four. What follows is a brief overview of each of these four styles.

The first style is that of *experienced faith*, found during the preschool and early childhood years. This is a time when children test one another and themselves, exploring, observing and copying, imitating the actions of one another. Therefore, language and experience are connected. For example, the words 'love' and 'trust' truly mean something through one's experience of the words.

The second style of faith is *affiliated faith* with three primary characteristics. The first deals with a sense of belonging: that all people need to feel as if they belong to a community and they have an opportunity to act like someone who truly belongs there, whether it's singing at the Christmas concert or dressing up as Esther at Purim. The second characteristic emphasizes the need to understand how important "religion of the heart" is. As Rev. Westerhoff explains: "In terms of faith, actions in the realm of the affections are prior to acts of thinking, which is why participation in the arts, whether it's drama, music, dance, painting, sculpture, storytelling, etc., is so essential to faith."[37] The third characteristic of affiliated faith is a sense of authority, which is the affirmation by the community of its story and way of life, which inspires its actions and activities.

The third style of faith is *searching faith*. This too has three characteristics, the first being doubt, or critical judgment. It is at this point, after childhood, when one has to come to terms with making the faith of one's community the faith of one's own, by critical thinking, searching and serious study. The second characteristic of searching faith is experimentation, where one examines alternatives to what one has learned, followed by the third aspect, which is commitment.

The fourth and final style of faith is *owned faith*, or what might otherwise be labeled conversion. It entails a major change in the way a person thinks and feels and more importantly, behaves. Because of the struggle that often ensues prior to this time, owned faith may appear as a clarity or enlightenment.

Given the amount of research available regarding developmental theory and having heard from several eminently qualified specialists regarding faith 'stages' (or styles or situations), we are somewhat prepared to take the next step: to come to some understanding of the definition of religion in the mode of Catholic sacramentality and a personal appreciation of religious identity as it relates to the sacrament of Baptism.

END NOTES

1. 1990 National Jewish Population Survey under the auspices of the Council of Jewish Federations

2. Joel Crohn, Ph.D., *Mixed Matches: How to Create Successful Interracial, Interethnic, and Interfaith Relationships* (New York: Fawcett Columbine, 1995), p. 13.

3. See *New York Magazine*, July 14, 1997, p. 35.

4. See the Jewish Outreach Institute article entitled "The Factors Behind the 52% Intermarriage Rate" at www.joi.org/library/research/index.shtml.

5. Ibid.

6. Egon Mayer, Ph.D., *Love and Tradition: Marriage Between Christians and Jews* (New York: Plenum Press, 1995), pps 282-283.

7. Crohn, *Mixed Matches*, p.150.

8. Barry Kosmin and Jeffrey Scheckner, *Highlights of the National Jewish Population Survey* (New York: Council of Jewish Federations, 1991)

9. See Everett Stonequist, *The Marginal Man: A Study in Personality and Culture Conflict* (New York: Russell & Russell, 1937) p. 145, the seminal work on anthropological sociology.

10. James H. Bossard and Eleanor S. Bell, *One Marriage, Two Faiths: Guidance on Interfaith Marriage* (New York: Ronald Press, 1957)

11. Louis Berman, *Jews and Intermarriage: A Study in Personality and Culture* (New York: Tomas Yoseloff, 1968) p. 209

12. Berman, Ibid. p. 221. Berman writes extensively on the work of Philip Rosten at Harvard.

13. Philip Rosten, *The Mischling: Child of the Jewish Gentile Marriage*, 1960. Unpublished honors paper submitted to the Department of Social Relations at Harvard University, Boston. p. 40

14. Ibid. p.55

15. Ibid. p.66

16. This data is excerpted from author sociologist Egon Mayer, Ph.D. *Children of Intermarriage: A Study in Patterns of Identification and Family Life* (New York: American Jewish Committee Publications, 1990) pp. 43-44

17. Egon Mayer, Ph.D. *Love and tradition – Marriage Between Christians and Jews.* p. 277.

18. Excerpted from an article in <u>Dovetail Magazine</u>, wherein the author details her research from her dissertation entitled *Mixed Up or Just Mixed? Adjustment of Children in Interfaith Families*

19. See Lee F. Gruzen, *Raising Your Jewish Christian Child* (New York: Newmarket Press, 1987) p. 229. While dated, this text is still one of the most readable, practical resources for interfaith families.

20. Judy Petsonk and Jim Remsen, *The Intermarriage Handbook – A Guide for Jews and Christians* (New York: William Morrow, 1988) p. 235

21. Ibid., p. 194

22. This is the overall tone taken by the author Susan Weidman Schneider in her book *Intermarriage: The Challenge of Living with Differences Between Christians and Jews* (New York: The Free Press, 1989)

23. Crohn, *Mixed Matches*, p.22

24. Elliot Abrams, *Faith or Fear – How Jews Can Survive in a Christian America* (New York: The Free Press, 1997), p. 136

25. Andrea King, *If I'm Jewish and You're Christian, What are the Kids?* (New York: UAHC Press, 1993), p. 3. There is a particular agenda to the case scenarios: those children raised Jewish are calm, clearheaded and religiously sound; those raised Christian come across as angry at their parents and confused as to their identity.

26. Rabbi Alan Silverstein, *It All Begins With A Date* (Northvale, New Jersey: Jason Aronson, Inc., 1995). The author takes the standard approach from the Conservative pulpit.

27. Kenneth Stokes (edit.), *Faith Development in the Adult Life Cycle* (William Sadlier, Inc, 1984) p. 47

28. Authors James Fowler and Sam Keen provide an excellent overview of the work of Eric Erickson, Jean Piaget and Lawrence Kohlberg, as well as their own definitive studies on the stages of faith over the life cycle in their book edited by Jerome Berryman entitled *Life Maps: Conversations on the Journey of Faith* (Waco, Texas: Word Books, 1978) p. 26

29. Ibid., p. 27

30. Ibid.,, pp. 30-33

31. In a private conversation with Professor L. Richard Bradley at the Hoboken, New Jersey symposium June 29-July 2, 1998 on "Mapping

Adult Faith Journeys" where he presented a discussion on the work of James Fowler.

32. See V. Bailey Gillespie, *The Experience of Faith* (Birmingham, Alabama: Religious Education Press, 1988), p.79

33. Ibid., p. 80

34. Ibid., p. 81

35. Ibid., p. 82

36. Rev. John H. Westerhoff, III, *Will Our Children Have Faith?* (New York: Seabury Press, 1976), p. 89

37. Ibid., p. 95

Sacramentality

Religions have done a very good job over the past several thousands of years delineating themselves in the manner of "<u>this</u> is who we are – we are not <u>that</u>", and often seeing those differences as a bad thing. Those of us who live in an interfaith marriage see those differences and honor them as a good thing, and having made that journey, think this is a sign of maturity in our spirituality. Hopefully this is a sign for a world (with the unspoken belief that it certainly is for our children) that we can come to look at our relationship with God, our beliefs originating from two different traditions, and recognize those as good. We struggle to remain authentic, that we wouldn't create a new religion without any particularities, or rituals or specifics: we cherish the notion that all of these pieces are important and should be part of a religious enterprise moving into a relationship with God.

Opening the newspaper or watching the news, one can see the strife, whether in Iraq, or Jerusalem, or Northern Ireland, or Rodgers Park, all in the name of religion. Again, religious immaturity declares "if you are different, that's a bad thing." While the suffering, destruction, and violence is horrific, one can only hope that a particular way of being religious in the world is dying, and we are moving towards a deeper spirituality: one that recognizes all the differences and the value of those differences, but also recognizes that we are trying to achieve the same thing on a spiritual level.

Somewhere along the lines of human existence, religion entered the picture. While there are a lot of definitions of religion to choose from, perhaps one that might work well here is the image of the raft at sea. We as human beings are headed for the shore, for union with the Divine. Religion is the raft we build. Unfortunately, we human beings get a little carried away with our raft-building sometimes, saying things like "Well, all the rafts need to look like mine" or "I really like the raft" while getting caught up in religious practice, and losing sight of where it's supposed to take us.

Here is a short definition of the Catholic raft: Catholicism is a way of living. (It should be noted that a definition of Judaism is similar: that is, to partner with God in the unfinished work of creation.)   The Latin word *'religare'* means to bind together, to tie up. Religion is supposed to make sense of our lives: all the rituals, practices, morals, and doctrines are supposed to give us the answers (or as the psalmist from the Old Testament revealed, "the whole world is full of God."). At the same time, religious understanding accepts the presence of mystery. Most religious traditions recognize that God is somewhere present in Creation, and therefore all creation we encounter has a bit of the mystery of God in it. Those viewing life through a Catholic lens know Catholicism is centered on Christ (remember the teachings *of* Jesus are very different from the teachings *about* Jesus. While we have some record of Jesus' preaching, the gospels come to us after a period of reflection, when those who followed his message had time to shape his identity.)   In addition to being Christ-centered, another important distinction about Catholicism is that it is lived in community: the church. Over centuries, many images of this community have been created: the people of God, the Mystical Body of Christ, the Temple of the Holy Spirit and so forth. It is important to recognize that the function of this church community is to acknowledge that the presence of God can be felt and experienced in all creation. The purpose of religion is not for God's sake after all; it's about transforming ourselves and transforming the world around us.

There is an old saying that the shortest distance between a human being and the truth is a story. With my apologies to the author, here is a story about Catholic sacramentality, the story of "The Temple of 10,000 Bells."

> *"There was a young man, a trader at the stock exchange who was extremely successful financially. However, along the way he started to question the meaning of his life, asking "is that all there is?" He started moving to a more spiritual level, seeking a more religious dimension in his life. Unsure of where to turn, he began to investigate a number of different religions and spiritual traditions, looking into the power of crystals, etc. but still was unsettled. In the course of his research and study, he came across a story which told of an ancient civilization that was situated somewhere on an island in the South Pacific, peopled by those especially attuned to a spiritual life. On this island they built a special*

44

temple and in the temple they installed 10,000 bells. It was said that if you were there when all 10,000 bells were rung, something in the nature of the sound was able to transport you to a divine union. They had found religious ecstasy. As you can imagine, he was intrigued by this story. However the story went on to say that somehow - whether it was by an earthquake, or a tidal wave or some other catastrophe, the temple was destroyed and the island sunk to the bottom of the ocean. But, the legend went on to say, people on a neighboring island insisted that if you went to the shore, you could still hear the 10,000 bells!

Well, that was enough for him. He took a few weeks' vacation from his job and made arrangements to stay on one of those neighboring islands in the vicinity of the island that had sunk into the sea.

When he arrived on the island, truly a beautiful tropical paradise, he walked to the middle of the village square looking for someone who appeared to be wise. Finding a village elder, he asked, "Is it true what I have read about the temple of 10,000 bells?" and was told in return, "Yes, it is true." He then asked what he needed to do, and the elder replied, "Go the beach." There was no prayer he needed to know, no ritual he needed to follow. And so he set off the next morning to make his way to the beach, walking through the jungle with simian activity above his head, birds singing, lush tropical flowers perfuming his journey. Coming through the vegetation, he walked onto the most exquisite white sandy beach, with clear warm waters lapping against his toes, and not a cloud in the sky. So he sat in the sand and listened, noting nothing more than the birds singing carried by the gentlest of breezes, the waves crashing from afar. Nothing happened, and so he returned to his room. The next day he went back to the same spot, where he encountered more of the same: the sound of the waves, the birds singing, and the monkeys playing. Nothing happened to him, day after day after day. In his frustration, one day he decided not to go his spot on the beach but rather to the bar, where he talked to the bartender. "Is this true, the story of the 10,000 bells, or is it just some lure to attract the *tourist trade?" The barkeeper assured him it was true; they could be heard, and he must return. And so he did, returning the same way to his spot on the beach through the dense thick sweet perfumed gardens, with birds and monkeys ever-present. Nothing happened.*

Now his vacation time was over and he needed to return home. He was frustrated that he had not found what he was looking for, having tried everything to get closer to the divine. So he packed his bags and as he gathered up his things, he thought he would miss what he had experienced and thought he would go one last time, as if to say good-bye to the spot. So he returned as he had for so many days previous, slowly walking through the jungle, listening to the sounds of the birds and the monkeys, taking in the dizzying fragrance from the flower blossoms, continuing on to the shore, where again the beach was pristinely beautiful, the water crystal clear. And he sat. And then, he heard the first bell.... then the second bell...then he heard the third, all the way to the 10,000th bell, when he did in fact reach religious ecstasy and a sense of union with the Divine."

This story is interesting on a number of levels, but might be used as an insight into Catholic sacramentality. If you want to find the Divine, to experience the Divine, you must throw yourself into the experience of life: You must throw yourself into creation! It's not the prayers and rituals necessarily, though along the way they will help, for they are the rafts. But to understand the Divine, to experience the Divine, you don't do an end run around Creation. The sacramental insight in Catholicism is simply that God is present in creation and every encounter with the creative world, with other people has the potential to be revelatory, to bring us closer into understanding and communion with God. For those that find the story unappealing or prefer a more traditional definition of sacramentality, here goes: it is the conviction that everything is capable of both embodying and communicating the Divine.

Within this context of sacramentality, the Catholic Church has determined there to be seven Sacraments (with a capital S). Most Catholics think that the number seven was established from the beginning, from the time of Jesus, when in fact there were a number of church councils during the middle ages (from 1200 to about 1500) which finalized the number to be such. In fact, during the development of Christianity, a lot of things were called sacraments: prayer, certain readings and scripture, even certain actions of people. It wasn't until the Middle Ages the church settled on these 7 moments as being instituted by Christ as high monuments of worship and unity.

In modern catechetical thinking, the Sacraments are grouped accordingly: those of Initiation (Baptism, Confirmation, Eucharist); those of Marriage and Holy Orders, which speak to commitment or vocational choice; and lastly Reconciliation (also called penance or confession) and the Anointing of the Sick (extreme unction or last rites). Baptism is obviously the initial moment of initiation into Christianity. While we will talk at some length in a later chapter about

the origins of Baptism, we can say for now in the early days of the church, it was an adult experience. When the first disciples of Jesus went out evangelizing new disciples, they were talking to adults, not to babies. After they were baptized, whoever was the leader of the community--a prototype, if you will, of the first bishops--would 'seal' their baptism through anointing with oil, which was followed by an invitation to join in a meal of communion called the Eucharist. This meant now you were a full member: you were incorporated into the order of Christianity.

Remember that the origin of the word 'sacrament' comes from the Latin word meaning 'a pledge of fidelity to your centurion', therefore originating from a mindset of militarism. The Greek word for these realities is "*mysterian*", the mysteries, so what we are celebrating are the great mysteries in life…birth, growth, communion, individual yet connected. Remember, there is no holy separate; it's holy *communion*, the being together a critical insight regarding Catholic Sacraments. To digress for a moment, there is a wonderful symbol in Eastern Christianity of the spoked wheel: God is the hub, and we are the spokes. We are all separate, that is God created me to be me, but we are all connected to the hub. If you want to get closer to the hub, to God, the only way you can do it is by getting closer to the other spokes---the other folks---as you move in! As you get closer to other people, you can't help but get closer to God. The dynamic of communion is we are separate as we revel in our individuality, but we remember we are connected to the central infinite. In addition, in the Catholic liturgy, we believe that not only is God present in the bread and wine, but also, that God is present in the person of the celebrant, in the word of God and in the assembled people: God is present in all of that.

Remember that sacraments are expressive and formative: they express a belief (for example at communion, we as Catholics believe that we share in a Communion with God); it's also formative, in that the power of the ritual somehow **transforms** us. Sacraments, therefore, address three human dynamics: identity, how we live out of that identity, and lastly, what do we do when things get broken. So it is the way it works with baptism: I recognize myself as a Beloved child of God. Let me suggest there are multiple baptisms. We do it once ritually, but any moment you are experiencing yourself as a beloved child of God, that's Baptism. As we will discuss in our next chapter, there are many moments where we are acting out of our identity as a beloved child: in the workplace, in our families, in our neighborhoods, and more often than we sometimes realize.

Identity

Right now at this time in your life, what would you say is your primary identity? Recently, I had the opportunity to ponder that question. Our family took a vacation, but realized in coming home we had made a mistake by not changing the message on the answering machine, notifying our callers that we would be away and unable to help them. There is nothing like turning the switch of the voicemail on to learn you have 80 messages! So grabbing my pencil, I sat and prepared to sort through them all: some were for my oldest daughter the teenager, from friends wanting to see the latest pirate movie; others were for the other children, friends wanting to make a date to swim, others wanting to get together to work on the latest guitar lesson; still others were for my husband.

However, as I sat and listened, I was struck by the distinct and separate realities of my life. I had already sorted out those calls addressing my role as both *wife* and *mother*; one call was from my mother wanting to see how the family was faring —I was the *daughter*; there was a call from a friend looking for information about an upcoming condo board meeting — I was the *neighbor*; my brother had called from California asking to see what the kids might like for their upcoming birthdays — I was the *sister*; someone from the interfaith dialogue called and I was the *counselor*. It struck me with an awareness of all the roles and identities that I hold, and that each of those identities has a way of being relationally connected. As I returned the calls, I heard myself in my different voices. As I began, I was conscious of how I spoke in each of those different roles: the voice I used to talk with my mom was not the same one I used as neighbor doing battle with the condominium association. The trick was not to transfer one voice to the other role! The realization was strong of just how many roles we play and how seamlessly we move in and out of them, almost without thought. In one moment we are in one voice, then reflexively into the next.

We begin to consider that deeper identity when we move more deeply into the spiritual realm of our lives.

Identity. The fact that we can move in and out of the identities we live out of and work out of means there is a deeper identity we have —one that is more than parent, or manager or doctor, or plumber or teacher. There is a common identity that each of us shares: deeper---more grounded---more central than our gender, than our roles in this life. We come to realize that part of the journey of life is trying to come to know and understand the identity that we move from within into the world that is consistent: that doesn't shift and flow; that is the primary sense of who we are.

When we talk about Baptism, we are talking about identity issues, and of course, Jesus. For the Christian, a sharing in Baptism is a sharing in the identity of Jesus Christ. Through Baptism we say we are given a 'share' in the identity of Jesus. But what was the identity of Jesus? In Scripture we learn that different people had many understandings of who they thought Jesus was: a carpenter, Mary's son, a rabbi, a prophet, a teacher, the Messiah. All kinds of identities, from his mother, from his disciples, from the crowds that gathered at that time to listen, were placed on him. But Jesus had to come to a recognition of his identity. By examining the story in scripture now, we can begin to see how this connects to the idea of Baptism in **this** time and age in a meaningful way.

In Luke we read

> *Now when all the people were baptized, and when Jesus also had been baptized and was praying, the heaven was opened, and the Holy Spirit descended upon him in bodily form like a dove. And a voice came from heaven "You are my Son, the Beloved, with you I am well pleased*
>
> Luke 3:21-22

Notice the term: **ALL** the people, not just some of the people, were baptized! Historically, John is calling all people to a new way of seeing and doing life ---calling people to an awareness, to a change in how they perceive their lives. Remember, at its origin, the image of Baptism was one of death and rebirth. Originally, when taken to the river to be baptized, the person doing the baptism would take the candidate and hold them under the water "In the name of the Father...." until they were just out of breath, rising to the surface gasping for air; "and of the Son..." again being held under until choking for breath; "and of the Holy Spirit..." in an almost near-drowning experience! The effect, of course, was that something had happened. It was a way of expressing that the side of you that was not Christ-conscious was dead. John was saying to those who led, to the teachers, that they had lost heart; they had lost their true identity as God's chosen ones.

We have come to learn that reading the scriptures is not the same as reading the daily newspaper! Scriptures are filled and laced with metaphor and meanings that are far deeper than those seen on the surface. In this story, the scriptures go on to tell us that Jesus is 30 years old when he is baptized and begins his work. Up to this point, the scriptures don't give us many details on his first 30 years of life. We don't know what he looked like, who he played with as a child, whether he threw a good curve ball or had a great jump shot! There are no details for us. But at 30 years old, something happens; something that signals a new beginning, getting in touch with that deeper identity that propels him into his mission and into life in a new way.

> You were being born into a new way of being: responding to life the way Christ responds to life. It was the end of one way of living and birth into a new way of being.

So Jesus follows the trend, as people are called to this renewal, or this change, or this turning around; goes into the waters, comes out of the waters and is at prayer. What do the scriptures mean when they say he is "at prayer"? Well, prayer is the way we make ourselves available to God. It's how we open ourselves to God's presence. It's not only about petition, it's about being in relationship, being open with raw honesty to God: that is, God can have his way with Jesus, with no defensiveness, no holding back--just pure communion with God. And as he is in prayer, the story tells us, the heavens opened. Did they actually, literally, historically open? Well, we think this is a metaphor meaning that God can communicate with Jesus in a way Jesus has never experienced before. And in this communication, what does God say? Does he say "Remember that time in the temple when you were twelve…" or "What the heck are you doing?" No, he says "You are my Beloved One; in you I am well pleased." Imagine the intensity of that experience! It reminds me of the intensity I felt when I first saw each of my children, and knew that I loved them. Think of the power that comes out of that moment. You move into life in a new way, with a new and deeper identity, living your daily life, knowing that you are the beloved of someone. Now imagine what the reality is to have the realization that you are the Beloved of God. You move into a whole new way of being.

So, that is the identity that Jesus discovers in this story of Baptism. There's forgiveness of sin, which means letting go of all those things which hold us back from believing that we are loved; there's prayer, open and vulnerable before the Divine, the communication that one is loved; and then there is a sharing in God's pleasure, that is, to know that you are loved.

What happens next? As soon as Jesus discovers this about himself, he is sent forth; he's empowered in mission and goes to the desert. That's an interesting place to go, filled with all this love! What's he going to find in the desert? Much like ourselves, we often discover our identity not just by insight of who we are, but by the realization of who we are *not*. So Jesus goes to the desert to discover what he doesn't need in his life.

> *Jesus, full of the Holy Spirit, returned from the Jordan and was led by the Spirit in the wilderness, where for forty days he was tempted by the devil. He ate nothing at all during those days, and when they were over he was famished. The devil said to him "If you are the Son of God command this stone to become a loaf of bread." Jesus answered him "It is written 'One does not live by bread alone.'"*
>
> Luke 4:1-4

You would think if you were the Beloved of God, if you were the Son of God, your physical needs would be met, that you would never be hungry. Wouldn't you imagine that would be the case? If I am the Son of God, and I am hungry, where is God? Shouldn't God provide for me? So what's discovered is that Jesus will be hungry: to be Beloved doesn't mean that you would not know hunger in your life. His response to the tempter is 'just because I am empty, unfulfilled physically, doesn't mean I'm not loved.' Are there not times when we are tested and left to wonder whether we are God's beloved? Jesus affirms "Yes, I am."

> *Then the devil led him up and showed him in an instant all the Kingdoms of the world. And the devil said to him "To you I will give their glory and all this authority; for it has been given over to me and I will give it to anyone I please. If you then worship me, it will all be yours." Jesus answered him "It is written 'Worship the Lord your God, and serve only him.'"*

Luke 4:5-8

When we think of God in our own fantasy, we think of Him as all-powerful, controlling all. And so if you are lacking in power, one might still ask "Am I still loved?" In my power*less*ness, am I still loved or do I question my identity as God's beloved in that moment? The Son of God should be all-powerful, and Jesus discovers in that temptation that he will not have power in terms of the world's notion of power, but rather the power of love (which we know is different than power and position in the world.).

And so on to the third temptation, up to Jerusalem at the pinnacle of the temple:

> *"Then the devil took him to Jerusalem, and placed him on the pinnacle of the temple, saying to him "If you are the Son of God, throw yourself down from here, for it is written 'He will command his angels concerning you, to protect you' and 'on their hands they will bear you up, so that you do not dash your foot against a stone.'" Jesus answered him "It is said 'Do not put the Lord your God to the test.'"*
>
> *Luke 4:9-12*

What's going on here? One would think if you were God's beloved, there would be an immunity from harm: you would be safe, you would never be hurt. You would emerge unscathed from dangerous situations. Jesus refuses this fantasy, knowing he will not be safe in the way the world understands safety. And even with that realization he will not question that he is the beloved of God. I am hungry, I am empty, am I loved by God? I am powerless and sometimes oppressed, am I still the beloved of God? I am unsafe, I am not immune from danger, am I still the beloved of God? Aren't those questions we ask ourselves in our prayer life: why do bad things happen to good people? If I am trying to do the best that I can, leading a life of love, why don't things always go my way? Why, if I try and try and try to be a good spouse, a good parent, a good person, why do things not always seem to work out? Are there not times in our own lives when we question whether God is involved in our life? This is the experience of Jesus. For the Christian, the story of Jesus is like taking a mirror to one's face, because the mysteries of life that he participates in, that we all as human beings participate in, are seen and revealed in the story of his life.

So, going back to the beginning and the issue of identity: Jesus is baptized, letting go of the past, experiences a discovery in prayer when he is most open to knowing that he is loved, and is empowered to share this pleasure of God with all people. But then, like any sense of identity which will need to be tested, we discover 'What does it mean to be the beloved of God?' It means that I will not have power in this world, I will be hungry, I will not always be safe--but also in those moments, I will not doubt who I am. That was the Baptism of Jesus.

How does the baptism of Jesus relate to us now? Just as Jesus discovered that his deeper identity was that he was the beloved of God, then for the Christian person of faith we come to understand that we are all the beloved of God, we are all the sons and daughters of God. Jesus then is the pathway that helps us come to the understanding and realization of this "good news." And that's why we baptize both children and adults into the news that we are God's pleasure: that we are loved without condition. Baptism celebrates what is, and what we sometimes fail to see: in holding up this child/adult, we come to see the face of God, this is the beloved one, the daughter and son of the Most High. Once we realize this deeper identity, we can move into the other roles of our life. As we grow into childhood and beyond, into the marketplace as a member of the workforce, the neighborhood, we carry a deeper sense of who we are. The knowledge of this identity has the power to transform who we are.

"To help recover the ritual life that sanctifies our existence, the dignity and power of the Image of God within us must be recovered. A legend of its hiddenness tells of a group of angels, who having heard that God intended to create the human being in God's own likeness, plotted to hide the

Image. One angel proposed hiding it on the pinnacle of the highest mountain. But a wiser angel pointed out that the human is an ambitious climber and would ascend the highest mountain. Another angel suggested that the Image be sunk beneath the deepest ocean. But this angel too was dissuaded from the plan when it was pointed out that the human is curious and would plumb the ocean and draw forth the hidden treasure. The shrewdest angel counseled that the Image should be hidden within the human beings themselves because it is the last place that they would be likely to look. For us, that must be the first place to look."

Harold Schulweis in *Finding Each Other in Judaism*

Rethinking Baptism

Holy Moments in Everyday Living

By Bill Huebsch

Almost no one can remember their baptism, which is not true for the other sacraments. Most of them leave a memorable impression on us: Who would forget their first time in the old confessional box? Or who has lost the memory of their first communion? We tend to really celebrate weddings and ordinations, making them unforgettable events in our lives. Confirmation, even though not very well understood, is a big family event. Even the "last rites" make a lasting impression, especially if you don't die after all. But baptism is forgettable, for the most part.

That's because we're baptized as babies rather than as adults. We have a sense of what it must have been like when we ourselves were baptized because we have a much better recollection of the baptisms of others than we do of our own. But the babies that we are baptizing will soon forget, just as we have.

So what happens at baptism that is so important? Is baptism something we do to babies in order to keep them from limbo? Or is there more to it than that?

It's important for us to talk about this. Baptism is, after all, the sacrament that, we are told, empowers us as "ministers." We keep hearing that Baptism is such a key, such a central, and such an essential sacrament. We're sure this is true, but since we can't remember, and we haven't been taught much, we feel a little in the dark. And, when it comes right down to it, and we honestly admit  how we feel and think about it, we have to admit that we do not experience baptism as anything but something we know happened "to us" once, when we were babies. In our heads we know it was important, but in our experience of life, it doesn't seem to matter that much.

The other sacraments are different: they're loaded with hoopla and schmaltz; we usually do them up in a big way! And they have an immediate impact in our lives: they're vital for us. But baptism is old hat; it happened for most of us so long ago that it doesn't seem to matter much now.

The only real contact that most of us have with our baptism in our adult lives is the renewal of baptismal promises that we do each year on Holy Saturday night. But it seems strange to us: "Do you reject Satan?" We mutter our way through the responses, provided we found the right page on the missalette, and it ends up that we aren't touched that deeply or profoundly. We're quite sure that we *do* reject Satan, but isn't there more to it than that?

There is some confusion about baptism today. We don't intend to clear that up here, but it *is* possible for us to get a clearer focus, a better footing, and a deeper appreciation for what did happen to us on the day we were baptized.

The confusion, at least in part, stems from the fact that there are two aspects to baptism which, when mixed together, seem troublesome. First, baptism is for adults: it is the end of a journey to faith in Christ; it is the final "yes," a faith-filled response, a decision to become a full member of the followers of Christ. In the early church, this meant years of study, and working a serious program of turning one's life over to Christ. It meant knowing the Scriptures, taking on a ministry in Christ's name, and making a solemn vow to remain faithful for life. It was a decision that only an adult could make, and it was not undertaken lightly.

But second, baptism is for kids. It is entering into a life, even as an infant, of being brought up in the church, a community of people committed to being for Christ. This means that the family, parish, circle of friends, and even strangers in church, become the seedbed for faith so that, from the earliest years of life, a child is "in Christ." Being "in Christ" means caring for one another without counting the cost;

listening to ourselves and accepting the truth we find there; reflecting and praying often, alone and with others; giving good news and food to the poor; proclaiming release to captives, recovery of sight to the blind, freedom to those bound in themselves, and proclaiming Jesus as Lord. Now this is not something a baby can do. But it is something that a baby can learn as a way of life only by being raised among other folks who have it as their goal.

So there we have it: baptism is for

adults, but baptism is for kids. How do we resolve this? Let's start with the kids and then move on to the adults, gaining perspective as we go.

Baptism is for kids. Being born is no fun, either for the mother or for child. For the mother there are months of waiting which end in painful moments of birthing. Even when the birthing is by surgery, there is pain and trauma. It's no picnic for the mother.

But our perspective here is going to be from the point of view of the child at birthing time.

The birthing begins really at conception, when the code of life contained in the fiber of the cells is set to determine a person. No one knows the exact time; it is a lonely moment for the child. A human being is being made and no one even knows it. A great shared power is at work: human and divine, but it works in secret. The child is at once unknown and yet fully at home.

And there, nestled in the warmth and darkness, something begins to stir. Cells multiply, not haphazardly, but not exactly planned. There in the comfort of that place, the first days and weeks and months of life are spent in preparation for birthing and whatever will follow. There has been no pain to bring this about--no suffering, no shedding of blood, as there will be at birthing. Rather, for most babies there is safety and security and waiting.

But then every good thing must come to an end, as they say, and birthing is inevitable. Comfortable as it may be, the time comes when discomfort is the way to birth.

And so it begins: the safety and security of the womb is replaced with the risks and responsibilities of the world. A child is born into a world, a place in history beset with needs and difficulties. That world, no doubt, is also filled with awe and wonder. But unlike the silent consent of conception, birthing is loud and confusing. In a word, birthing raises a ruckus!

> We sort of believed that babies were born in sin. That's an awful thought, that a baby is born in sin, but thankfully it's more a popular belief than an official teaching of the church.

Our topic here, we must remember, is not birthing but baptism. The child is born unbaptized, that is our point; and what that means for us is our next concern. The child is born with original sin.

Remember original sin? Jim Lopresti has said that original sin has been "closed" ---for repairs! There is a bit of misunderstanding about original sin that we should clear up in order to fully understand baptism.

When we were kids going to catechism class, many of us were taught that every human being at the time of birth was somehow guilty of sin. We sort of believed that babies were born in sin. That's an awful thought, that a baby is born in sin, but thankfully it's more a popular belief than an official teaching of the church. This notion that babies are born in sin had a loose connection to the religious idea that sex is a sin: sex and reproduction and all that stuff.

We've had a hard time finding much divine glory in this, but more and more we can see that God gave us sex and fruitfulness as the crowning moment of all creation. "Be fruitful and multiply and fill the earth." All of this was God's idea, and it must be good.

But that thought aside for the moment, we must insist as our starting point that babies are not born in sin. They are not personally guilty of anyone else's sins either. But, mysteriously, they do have an inner condition, common to all humans, which renders them subject to sin. This inner condition is not itself a freely chosen rejection of God, but rather this: we are, all of us, subject to darkness. We do not know ourselves; we do not love perfectly; we do not choose truth without pain, good without difficulty, right without doubt. There is something going on inside us, which, as Paul said it, makes us choose the very things we do not want to choose. It is not that we are born evil, but that we are born with the possibility of choosing evil.

The inner human condition that gives rise to this possible choice of darkness and sin, that inner condition, is our original sin. It isn't a sin in the sense that it is a freely chosen rejection of God, the kind of sins we commit as adults. Really, it is more accurate to say that it resembles sin and gives rise to the possibility of sin. It is, in a sense, an admission that as human beings, we have lost our innocence.

The story of Adam and Eve helps us understand this. In that story, the people were given many gifts, everything they needed for life. In a sense, that time was a womb time, when everything was provided and they did not need to worry. They had all that, but instead of using the gifts of the garden for good, for relating, for sharing with one another, they chose to be selfish. That was their sin.

The story of Adam and Eve is true, literally true, but it is true about us, not about them. The choice to be selfish or generous, sinful or graceful, in darkness or in light ---that is the awful choice that we must make.

Now we know that no baby born only days earlier can make such a choice. We do not believe or teach that such a child is in sin. But they are born with that inner condition which makes it necessary for them to face that awful choice between light and darkness.

Here, though, is the real key to baptism--because that's not all babies are born with, and it's not even the most important thing. Babies are also born with grace.

Grace is a power we receive from God, a power that enables us to know ourselves in ways that animals don't. It's an orientation towards God that is present in each of us from the very beginning. That grace is part of being human. Their very birth itself is a moment of grace. Like all humans, they do not have at birth all the grace they need; but they are born in grace, there's no doubt about it.

Baptism celebrates that: It celebrates the "other condition" that is present there, the condition of grace.

Baptism empowers that child to choose truth, goodness, beauty and right. The ancient ritual of pouring water unites that child with the spiritual forces of the ages in a history-long struggle to overcome darkness with the light of the Great Spirit. By itself, the child and the world do not stand a chance. By itself, the child is isolated and alone. Baptism, we might say, awakens within the child the grace implanted there by God to be united with Christ, and thereby united with the body of Christ as well. Baptism initiates that child into the church.

> **Baptism empowers that child to choose truth, goodness, beauty and right. The ancient ritual of pouring water unites that child with the spiritual forces of the ages in a history-long struggle to overcome darkness with the light of the Great Spirit.**

But there is more. There is a deep inner power released at the pouring of the water, but there is also something happening to the others present. Baptism doesn't affect only the newly baptized. The others present at this moment find themselves mysteriously linked to a great spiritual force. They are, in a sense, refreshed themselves in their own inner life.

So babies are born in the state of grace, but they are also born without grace. They are born in the state of grace because of Christ's life. That life, once and for all, empowers us to live ourselves, as he did, in the energy of God. But they are born without grace because we are human after all: and as Christ has shown, we must pass through death in order to be fully alive. So this child, having all the possibility of full life, must also cope with a difficult world.

Babies, after all, *are* born into a sinful world. And they are born with that awful power to choose between life and death. So the other side of baptism is that it brings us first and foremost into a group of people who are also facing the same terrible choice. If only we didn't have that freedom!

But we do and we're glad of it, really. And in just the same way that we learn, through the story of the garden, about the pull from both sides, so we in our day also find both the light of Christ and the darkness of sin appealing. Baptism, besides giving us an inner power, also gives us one another. So baptism, really, is for adults.

Baptizing babies is easy, but living a baptized life as an adult is not. This part of what we have to say here will make us uncomfortable, I think, because it pushes us to take seriously what we do to our children.

Perhaps more than any other, baptism is a sacrament that stays with us. It's a sacrament that continually forms us and molds us.

I don't know how long it's going to take us to figure out that we need one another. Children understand this pretty well, and older people do too. But it's the big, independent bunch in the middle years that forget this. It's those folks who are financially independent, socially secure, domestically settled and generally able to take care of themselves. It's those folks who think they can also be emotionally independent and spiritually private. It's them, those other guys and gals, those folks: but really, it's *we*, isn't it? We continually choose to go it alone, to be unilateral, to repeat the story of the garden. What's our problem? Can't we get it into our heads that being human means being together? Every Sunday, all over the country, we have churches full of people who, even though they're in church, are still trying to go it alone. Even though we are all baptized, still we are alone.

The story from Genesis of the man and woman in the garden is a story of people like us whose relationship was ruptured by selfishness, greed, a love for power and a unilateral way of living. Those ruptured relationships are at the core of our own sin. They are also at the core of poverty, war, sickness, meanness, terrorism, loneliness and pain. But we don't have to live like that. We do have another choice.

We have too long been taught, I think, that what happens at baptism is complete. We have been taught that, once we're baptized, it's over, that we've got all we're gonna get from God. But that's not true. Perhaps more than any other, baptism is a sacrament that stays with us. It's a sacrament that continually forms us and molds us. Being baptized into Christ is being united with him in that struggle to undo what was first done in the garden. It means that we become relational.

It means, in short, that we become part of one another, learn to care for one another, provide generously for one another, share ourselves freely. It means that our first priority cannot be getting rich, or famous, or smart, or powerful, or pleasureful. Our first priority becomes that of Christ, to join with others in order to love them.

So even though we're baptized as babies, we still must give our adult selves to Christ. And we do that by giving our adult selves to one another in community. But how long will it take us to realize this? How long will it take us to turn to one another, not for profit, not for pleasure, not for power but in love? How long will it take us to realize that this deep longing for affection and love that we have, this longing for companionship and care, this longing is a longing for Christ? It is the deer that longs for running streams; it is us.

There is a story in the gospel that brings all this to light in a very poignant and stirring way. It is the story of a blind man, and it's in

the gospel of Mark. In this story, this guy is sitting along a road and the text tells us that he is a blind beggar. Now, as soon as you hear that, you probably say to yourself that this must be a story about someone else. Surely, it couldn't be a story about you! After all, you aren't a blind beggar, are you? Well, listen up! This is a story about us, about being blind the way we are and about begging the way we do. You see, the thing about being blind is that you can't see what you can't see. So we are sometimes blind and don't even know it, and that's the kind of blindness that this story is about, the kind that you and I have.

The story says that this blind guy was sitting alongside the road. He really wasn't going anywhere--he was stalled, stopped, and staid. And his name was Bartimaeus.

That name is significant: it means, literally, "son of fear." That's us, okay. How often has fear stopped us, parked us alongside the road of life? How often have we failed to go the extra mile with someone because we feared the involvement? How often have we been silent, even with the person we are married to, because we are afraid?

This gospel writer understood fear, and was writing to an audience that lived in fear of their very lives. Only a few verses earlier, the gospel writer tells us a story about Jesus and the apostles. They are talking among themselves, some of the apostles, about who would have glory in Jesus' kingdom. They're kind of dumb, those guys, because they don't understand the kind of kingdom Jesus was announcing. So Jesus tells them, "You don't know what you're talking about. You must be *baptized* as I have been baptized," he tells them "and that baptism will render you a servant." Servanthood, Jesus had tried to explain to them, involves giving up your life. The apostles wanted a shortcut to glory; they wanted to bypass the pain of death. They feared the cost of being a follower of Jesus.

But getting back to poor old Bartimaeus. There he sat, full of fear, stopped dead in his tracks and going nowhere and wearing a heavy cloak. And here we sit, afraid to turn in love to one another. The very thing we want most in life, to have real caring and loving, is also the thing we fear the most. The ache we feel deep inside us, in our most honest moments, is the ache to be held emotionally and physically by someone who cares--and yet we refuse to allow that to happen because the fear is so great.

But when Jesus came walking along, when he entered his life in the dramatic way that Jesus can, Bartimaeus realized he had a chance and he began to cry out for all his worth! "Jesus! Help me!" And sure enough, Jesus heard his cry and called the old guy over to him. Then the text says something interesting. Bartimaeus, it says, threw off his mantle. He threw off the monkey on his back, the stone around his neck, the garbage he'd been carrying that had him weighed down. He threw off, in a word, his fears, and he came to Jesus.

What does this mean? It means that he gave up his grip on himself and came to realize that he needed to be in Christ, which means he needed the love and affection we mentioned earlier. Baptism is our entry into that, but often it really is merely a forgotten ritual without lasting influence in our lives. What it means to "reject Satan," what it means to be in Christ, is to reject isolation and aloneness and accept community. We do that, to accept community by turning to one another to share our lives together, not in some safe, antiseptic way, but in sharing: intimacy, honesty, openness, kindness, and love. In a word, we enter into Christ's community when we take the real risk of donating ourselves to one another. So Bartimaeus threw off his mantle and went to Christ. What did Christ say to him? He asked him a question: "What do you want from me?" Jesus asked.

And what do you suppose Bartimaeus said to Jesus? "I want to see," he said, "Please, I want to see." I want to see what I am blind to. I want to see myself. This text summarizes in a few brief lines what must have been a great relationship between Jesus and this man. The gospels do that, but we can surmise from this that Jesus did help this man to see what he could not see because the story concludes by telling us that he was made well. And then it tells us as well that, once he'd received his sight, he was no longer parked, no longer stalled alongside the road. The text is explicit in telling us that now he followed Jesus "on the way" down the road.

This is our story, and it's the story of the baptized. We're stopped short by our blindness, by that inner condition that renders us sinful sometimes. But because of Christ, with whom we began to live at baptism, we are made to see, we are restored to health, we are made whole and therefore, made holy.

The point of this story is the point of our story: we could cross the barren desert without dying of thirst; we could wander far in safety without losing our way; we could speak our words in foreign lands, and all would understand: we could see the face of God and live! We need not be afraid to enter our baptismal commitment. We need not be afraid to put on Christ by turning to one another. We need not be afraid because, although we suffer an inner condition of weakness, more powerful than that will always be our inner condition of grace.

From the text of the same name. Reprinted with permission by the author. Originally published by Twenty-Third Publications, Mystic Conn. 1989

An Introduction to the
Hebrew Rites of Initiation

*God also said to Abraham: "On your part, you and your
descendants after you must keep my covenant throughout
the ages. This is my covenant with you and your
descendants after you that you must keep: every male
among you shall be circumcised. Circumcise the flesh of
your foreskin, and that shall be the mark of the covenant
between you and me. Throughout the ages, every male
among you, when he is eight days old, shall be circumcised,
including houseborn slaves and those acquired with money
from any foreigner who is not of your blood. Yes both the
houseborn slaves and those acquired with money must be
circumcised. Thus my covenant shall be in your flesh as an
everlasting pact. If a male is un-circumcised, that is, if the
flesh of his foreskin has not been cut away, such a one shall
be cut off from his people; he has broken my covenant."*

Genesis 17:9-14

And so, with those words, the Almighty forged his contract
with his beloved people: He would be their God and they would be His
people, Israel.

Yet historically, circumcision had been practiced in antiquity
among peoples other than the ancient Hebrews, though to what degree
and for what reasons we are uncertain. In Egypt, archeologists have
unearthed murals that detail the custom as a rite of passage into
puberty; Herodotus speaks of it, telling us that the Phoenicians and
Syrians were circumcised (yet certain mummies are not circumcised). It
is widely accepted that the Arabs in the ancient world also were
circumcised and to this day some African tribes practice circumcision,
with its meaning taken as a rite of initiation into the clan.[1]

While we cannot hope to understand the intent of primitive
peoples in regard to circumcision, social anthropologists have advanced
a number of theories as to the significance of this ritual. There are three
that are most often noted, which we can highlight briefly here. The first
theory is that it was performed for physical reasons (including health),
possibly as a preparation for marriage. The second hypothesis is one

that considers circumcision as a form of sacrifice, that is a part being "offered up" instead of the whole (though Hebrew scholars are doubtful that this applied in the case of the Hebrew peoples). The last and third premise is that circumcision was an act of initiation into a) the duties of man/adulthood and b) into a nation or tribe.[2] It is also doubtful that it was to be a tribal 'mark', as the mark would be hidden from view! It is interesting to note that the Hebrew words for *bridegroom, father-in-law* and *son-in-law* are all derived from the same root word, *hatan,* which means "to circumcise" in Arabic![3]

And then, as we read above, for the Hebrew peoples at the time of Father Abraham, circumcision was commanded by God, the ritual now taking on religious significance. Rabbi Joseph Teluskin poses the question why God chose circumcision as the "visible sign" of his covenant with the men of Israel. He answers us by stating "the Bible offers no explanation; however it is most likely....that it is a powerful symbolic way for a boy or a man to **express his willingness to subjugate himself to God's will.**"[4]   So what had possibly been a rite of passage for marriage or puberty, circumcision was now to be performed from that time on at eight days after birth as commanded. Author Thomas Cahill, in his book *The Gift of the Jews: How a Tribe of Desert Nomads Changed the Way Everyone Thinks and Feels* (Anchor Books: 1998) adds a similar take on the issue of why. "It is impossible for any man to forget …his own personal life force. By this covenant, the children of Abraham will be virtually unable to forget the god who never forgets them and who in his growing splendor and exclusivity appears less and less like a portable amulet to be rubbed for good luck. This god is losing the guardian-angel aspect of the Sumarian patronal gods and is turning into---God. To us, this covenant may appear barbaric. But within the rigid simplicities of Canaan and Mesopotamia, this "covenant in your flesh," this permanent reminder, makes perfect sense."[5]

There is also the metaphorical use of the word which we find in scripture: in Jeremiah (9:24), we see the 'uncircumcised heart' is a heart that cannot understand (*For all these nations, like the whole house of Israel, are uncircumcised in heart*); again in Jeremiah (6:10) we learn of the 'uncircumcised ear' which is an ear that does not listen (*To whom shall I speak? Whom shall I warn and be heard? See! Their ears are uncircumcised, they cannot give heed)* and finally of 'uncircumcised lips', which are those that cannot speak (Ex. 6:12, 30).

Initially it was the task of the child's father to perform the ritual. Later on, the rite of circumcision was performed by an observant Jew (a man) trained for the practice, called a *mohel.* The rite of circumcision, in Hebrew the *brit* (or **covenant**) *milah* (**circumcision**) is performed by a mohel under certain guidelines. For example, it is not appropriate to have a physician or surgeon perform the circumcision while a Rabbi recites the blessings nearby. Additionally, the brit should take place on the eighth day after birth, even if it is the Sabbath or Yom Kippur, so sacred is  the practice (remember, however, that in Jewish tradition, a day is counted from the onset of *night,* not midnight. So for example, if a child is born on a Tuesday night, the brit would take place the following Wednesday morning!). It is only in cases where the child is too weak, sick, or premature and the procedure considered a risk to the health of the baby that the ceremony is delayed. Other guidelines recommend that while the brit can be performed in the presence of just the father, it is preferable to have a *minyan,* that is ten men, including the mohel and the dad.[6] Interestingly, the word minyan, literally meaning "a number," is in reference to the ten scouts who brought back to Moses their report of their expedition to the land of Canaan (according to rabbinic scholars). It is also customary at the ceremony to set aside an empty chair, reserved for the prophet Elijah. Just as we remember Elijah at Passover with an offering from a cup of wine, we honor his presence with an empty chair, as Elijah defended the ritual of circumcision in ancient times to make sure the link to God continued from the word and time of Abraham and Sarah until now. Mohel Bill Barrows of Chicago says the intensity of the brist for him is not the circumcision, which most people focus on. Rather the critical moment is "when we ponder what Elijah stood for most and why he is here at each brist: that deep within each of us is the potential that we might be the one to bring God's greatest hope, that of world peace."[7]

At the ceremony, the following benediction is offered by the child's father:

Baruch ata adonai elohainu melech ha-olam asher kidshanu b'mitzvotav
v'tzivanu
L'hakhniso bivrito shel Avraham avinu.

which translates

> Blessed art Thou, Lord our God, King of the Universe who
> has sanctified us with His
> Commandments and commanded us to bring him into the
> Covenant of our father Abraham.

All of the guests answer with a resounding "Amen" and state
K'shem she-nikhnas labrit, ken yikanes "Torah, u-l'hupah u-l'maasim tovim
meaning

> Just as he entered the Covenant, so may he enter into a
> study of Torah, into marriage and into the performance of good
> deeds.

As with many Jewish celebrations, a joyful celebration would follow, with food and drink marking the experience as a "religious feast."

There is another beautiful ceremony for male children within the Jewish tradition, which is the redemption of the first-born son.[8]

It was originally intended that the first-born sons constitute the priesthood and be consecrated to the service of the Lord. In Numbers 8:17 we read

> For every first born among the children of Israel is mine... I
> consecrated them to myself on the day that I smote every first born in
> the land of Egypt.

Again in Exodus 13:11 the Lord speaks to Moses, saying

> When the Lord your God has brought you into the land of
> the Canaanites, which he swore to you and your fathers he
> would give you, you shall dedicate to the Lord every son
> that opens to womb; and all male firstlings of your animals
> shall belong to the Lord...Every first-born son you must
> redeem. If your son shall ask you later on 'What does this
> mean?' you shall tell him 'With a strong hand the Lord
> brought us out of Egypt, that place of slavery. When
> Pharaoh stubbornly refused to let us go, the Lord killed

every first-born in the land of Egypt, every first-born of man and beast. That is why I sacrifice to the Lord everything of the male sex that opens the womb, and why I redeem every first-born of my sons.

In the wake of Israel's backsliding in the incident of the Golden Calf, where the first-born showed themselves to be unworthy of the priestly office, when only the tribe of Levi was not guilty of this sin, the Levites were chosen to replace the first-born in the service of the sanctuary, with Aaron and his descendants, all Levites, becoming the priests (kohamin). Again, in Numbers we read

Thus shall you set the Levites apart from among the children of Israel; and the Levites shall be Mine…in place of all the first issue of the womb, of all the first born of all the children of Israel….Now I take the Levites instead of every first-born among the children of Israel.

Numbers 8: 14, 16, 18)

Since initially the first-born had been the ones whose lives were to be consecrated to the lifelong service of the Lord, they now had to be formally redeemed from that role and the redemption money paid to the kohen. The ceremony where this redemption takes place is called a *Pidyon Haben.*

And so, a Pidyon is celebrated if
✓ The child is the first born of his mother,
✓ The child is a male,
✓ The father is NOT a kohen or a Levi, nor is the mother a daughter of a kohen or a Levi

If any of the above three conditions are missing, the ceremony is NOT performed.

There are additional guidelines for the ceremony to proceed:
✓ A first born male child who is born *after* a miscarriage does NOT require a ceremony;

✓ A first born male child born via a Caesarian section does NOT require a ceremony;

✓ A kohen is required to perform the ceremony – even if the most gifted rabbinic scholar is present and he is NOT a kohen, he is not qualified to officiate at the service.

Remember, the idea upon which the redemption of the firstborn is based is that the first and the best of everything we earn or possess is due the Lord as an offering – not the mediocre or the leftovers!

The ceremony itself is a simple one. The father brings his firstborn son before the kohen and informs him of the same. The kohen then asks, "What do you prefer, to give me your son or to redeem him?" The father answers "to redeem him"; then, holding five pieces of silver currency in his hand, the father recites

Baruch ata adonai elohainu melech ha-olam asher
kidshanu b'mitzvotav V'tzivanu al pidyon haben

Blessed art Thou, Lord our God, King of the Universe who has sanctified us with his commandments and commanded us concerning the redemption of the firstborn son.

The *sheheheyanu* is then recited:
Baruch ata adonai elohainu melech ha-olam sheheheyanu
v'keey'manu v'hee-gee-anu lazman hazed

Blessed art Thou, Lord our God, ruler of the Universe who has kept us in life and Sustained us and enabled us to reach this day.

The father gives the money to the kohen, who takes it and passes it over the head of the child, saying, "This is in place of this child...". He then recites the Priestly Benediction over the baby and ends the service with the blessing over a cup of wine.

It is interesting to note what the writer called Luke says in the New Testament regarding the baby, Jesus:

When eight days were completed for his circumcision, he was named Jesus, the name given him by the angel before he was conceived in the womb... When the days were completed for their purification according to the law of Moses, they took him up to Jerusalem to present him to the Lord just as it had been written in the law of the Lord, "Every male that opens the womb shall be consecrated to the to the Lord" and to offer sacrifice of "a pair of turtledoves or two young pigeons" in accordance with the dictate in the law of the Lord.

Luke 2:21-24

The editors of the new *American Bible* (1990) point out that Luke makes it clear from the above that the family of Jesus was very much a part "of the people of Israel...The presentation of Jesus in the temple depicts the parents of Jesus as devout Jews, faithful observers of the law of the Lord."[9]

And so, finally, we move to the naming of a child. From the earliest times among primitive peoples, the name of something symbolizes the essence of it: to name something is to know it and consequently "to have power over it."[10] According to author Anita Diamant in *What to Name Your Jewish Baby,* "Like Adam's appointed task of giving names to all living things in Eden, naming is an exercise in power and creativity."[11] Names found in the Hebrew Scriptures were inspired in various ways: it could be by a circumstance of birth (i.e. being the fourth daughter or being born on a rainy day); a name could be of an animal or a plant or flower (i.e. such as a bee, or a dove, or a viper); names could be chosen that contained a divine title, expressing a religious idea (i.e. the mercy of God, or the help expected from the Almighty); names were chosen to honor a grandfather, or great-grandfather; and lastly, a name could be chosen then changed, often reflecting a change in personality or a change in one's fate (i.e. Jacob became Israel for wrestling with God).[12] Tradition was that the child was given a name at birth.

The idea upon which the redemption of the first born is based is that the first and the best of everything we earn or possess is due the Lord as an offering---not the mediocre, or the leftovers!

In contemporary Judaism, baby boys are named during their *brit milah,* or circumcision (although it's interesting to note that this custom was first documented in New Testament times, in Luke 1:59 referring to John the Baptist and again Luke 2:21 at the birth of Jesus: *When they came on the eighth day to circumcise the child, they were going to call him Zechariah after his father* and *When eight days were completed for his circumcision, he was named Jesus, the name given him by the angel before he was conceived in the womb*). A female child traditionally is named in the synagogue the week following her birth when her father is called up to the Torah, which we will see in just a moment. There is an interesting difference between those Jews of European descent (Ashkenazic Jews) and those from the Mediterranean (Sephardic Jews). The Ashkenazic Jews **rarely** name a baby after someone alive, but rather honor the name of a deceased relative (this probably stems from superstition centuries old to avoid having the Angel of Death take the baby by mistake, rather than the aging relative for which it was named). The Sephardic Jews, on the other hand hold no such fear and will often name a baby in honor of someone still alive.[13]

The naming ceremony in the synagogue begins with the Rabbi saying

> *God and Creator, happy parents have come into your presence to voice the longings of their hearts in prayer. Give them the wisdom to teach their children to be faithful to the heritage of the Household of Israel that he (she) may grow up with the knowledge that You are always near to him (her), guiding and sustaining him (her). Keep open the eyes of his (her) spirit, that he (she) may be ever conscious of the beauty and wonder of your world. And let him (her) learn to love the goodness that is in man and woman, that he (she) may ever nourish the goodness that has been implanted within him (her). Though none can escape sorrow and pain, we humbly ask for him (her) the courage to face evil, the faith to transcend it, and the strength to subdue it. Grant him (her) health of mind and strength of body, that he (she) may enjoy fullness of years and live to do your will in faithfulness. Amen.*

The parents respond by reciting the *Sheheheyanu* and praying for their child:

> *May we show our gratitude to You by leading our son in the way of righteousness. Teach us so to guide and instruct him, that he may grow up to be loyal to Judaism and a worthy member of the Jewish community.*

If the parents have given birth to a daughter, the following prayer is offered by the parents:

May we show our gratitude to You by leading our daughter
in the ways of righteousness. Teach us so to guide and
instruct her, that she may grow to be loyal to Judaism and a
worthy member of the Jewish community.

Accordingly, the Rabbi will bless the child, saying

May the One who blessed our fathers, Abraham, Isaac and
Jacob (our mothers, Sarah, Rebekah, Leah and Rachel)
bless this child with life and health. May he (she) be a joy to
his (her) parents. May he (she) live to bring honor to the
House of Israel. Blessing to humanity, and glory to the
name of God.

Now in the presence of loved ones, we give to this child the
name (.............). Let it become a name honored and
respected for wisdom and good deeds. May God's blessing
rest upon this child now and always.

The ceremony comes to a conclusion with the recitation of the Priestly Benediction and the passing of a cup of wine among the guests, with a few drops offered to the baby.

When selecting a Hebrew name for one's child, what is most important is that you choose it carefully. There are very few religious guidelines in selecting a name, yet there are a number of resources to use, both in book form and on the internet, which are listed in the appendix of this book.

What follows next is the ceremony in which our children are welcomed and blessed within our Catholic and Jewish traditions. Please know this ceremony is not for every family: in same cases, you may decide you are not ready; you may choose to celebrate just a Jewish ceremony (with a Catholic presence) or just a Baptism (with a Jewish presence). Whatever your decision, choose to make an authentic one, with an open and honest heart, and be prepared when you say "Amen" to mean it.

END NOTES

1. See Roland DeVaux, *Ancient Israel: Social Institutions, Vol. I* (New York: McGraw Hill, 1965)

2. See J.P. Hyatt's essay on circumcision found in *The Interpreters Dictionary of the Bible, Vol. I* (New York: Abingdon Press) p. 631

3. Private conversation with Hebrew scholar Dr. Rachel Dulin, Professor of Bible at Spertus Institute and DePaul University, Chicago

4. See Rabbi Joseph Teluskin, *Biblical Literacy* (New York: William Morrow & Co., 1997) p. 409

5. Thomas Cahill, *The Gift of the Jews (How a Tribe of Desert Nomads Changed the Way Everyone Thinks and Feels)* (New York: Nan Talese/Anchor Books, 1998) p. 72

6. Please see Rabbi Hayim Halevy Donin's book *To Be A Jew – A Guide to Jewish Observance in Contemporary Life* (New York: Basic Books, 1972). A good deal of material there was utilized regarding the birth rituals for children, pages 271-275. For a copy of the complete service, a Jewish prayer book should be consulted.

7. Private conversation with Mohel and Physician Bill Barrows regarding the intensity of the brit milah to him

8. Ibid., p. 276

9. See the footnote to the text of Luke 2:22, detailing the relationship of the family of see to the Mosaic tradition. *The New American Bible* (New York: Catholic Book Publishing, 1987) p. 101

10. R. Devoux, p. 44

11. Originally published in the book *What to Name Your Jewish Baby* by Anita Diamant (Summit Books, 1989), re-cited on the internet at http://judaism.com/library/weekly/aa013000a.htm in the article "Naming Your Jewish Baby", February 2002. Another excellent book by the same author is *The New Jewish Baby Book: Names, Ceremonies and Customs – A Guide for Today's Families* (Jewish Lights Publishing, 1994)

12. Ibid.

13. Originally cited on the internet at http://www.ritualr.com/hebrewnames.htm, in the article "Jewish Baby Names", February 2002

A Celebration of Welcome
and Initiation for Children

The Rite of Baby Naming and Baptism

(Our actions at this time of gathering will help set the tone for the celebratory event. Preparation and hospitality are key, as families and friends arrive for the ceremony. Special attention of welcome should be given to parents with their children, making sure they are comfortable. Along with program booklets, an insert will have been prepared containing the Hebrew names of the children, the names of the parents and Godparents and those of the readers.)

GATHERING RITE

Gathering Psalm 131, Prayed Together

Refrain: Like a little child in its mother's arms, my soul will rest in you.

Verse: My heart is not proud, my eyes do not seek the ways from above, the things that are great. The marvels beyond are not what I need, for you are my peace. (Refrain)

Verse: Quiet and still, my soul is calm, in your sweet embrace, like mother and child, my hope is in you: my heart is full, for you are my peace. (Refrain)

Verse: As the deer that longs for the stream, my soul longs for you, to see your face. To you I will sing and offer my thanks, for you are my peace. (Refrain)

GREETING AND WELCOME

Priest: This celebration is a time of great hope and joy for the People of God, of whom we here are a sign. For today, by the bestowal of Hebrew names and through the waters of new life, we welcome these children into our families and faith communities. Let us remember this moment as a time when we are aware of the wonders that God continues to work among us.

Rabbi: As people of faith, we are called to live lives of love, justice and service to humankind. These parents gather us to witness to their desire that their children grow in the faith and traditions which have been handed down to us through the ages in our communities of faith.

And so, we give thanks for arriving at this moment; please join me in the recitation of the Sheheheyanu:

Baruch Atah Adonai Eloheynu Melech Ha-o'lam Sheheheyanu, V'Kee-y'manu, V'Hee-gee-anu Lazman Ha-zeh

Blessed is the Lord our God, Ruler of the Universe, for giving us life, for sustaining us and enabling us to reach this day.

Blessed is the Lord our God, Ruler of the Universe, whose love and kindness extend to all the world.

Parents: Oh God, for the gift of these children we give you thanks and praise. Make us worthy of the privilege and responsibility of parenthood.

BABY NAMING: THE BESTOWING OF HEBREW NAMES

(Again, preparation for the families is very important. The families will have had the opportunity to establish the name they will bestow upon their child and to learn from the Rabbi the significance of that name. In the U.S. it is common to give a child both an English name and a Hebrew name, which may or may not be the same. In addition, the Rabbi will have knowledge of that information prior to the ceremony and be prepared to speak with surety to each family and the community gathered. This information will be included in the program insert.).

Rabbi: And so parents, I ask you, what names do you bestow upon your child?

Parents respond with the name of the child

Rabbi: And in whose honor is he/she named?

Here the parents share the significance of the chosen name
Rabbi offers commentary on each of the chosen names

WELCOMING OF GODPARENTS

Priest: Parents, who are they that you have chosen to serve as Godparents for your children?

Parents introduce and present the Godparents of their children

> Godparents, you have been chosen by these parents as representatives of their families and the faith community. They see in you so much that they love, respect and admire. They invite you to begin a very special relationship with their children, to be there for them at the important moments of their lives. You are to be an encouragement to their parents and particularly to assist in their growing to be faithful people, people that are aware of God's presence in their lives, people that are aware of the goodness in life. And so, Godparents I ask you, are you ready to support these parents through your encouragement and prayer, and by your presence in the lives of these children?

Godparents: We are ready and willing.

Rabbi: We have welcomed these children through the bestowal of Hebrew names and through signs of greeting and welcome. We now listen to readings from our Sacred Scriptures.

THE FIRST READER IS CALLED FORTH FROM THE GATHERING

SHARING OF THE WORD

(Prior to the ceremony, two readers will have been chosen and each given a specific reading. Readers should have had the opportunity to prepare their reading and proceed with clarity, enthusiasm and conviction.)

First Reading: Isaiah 11

> A shoot shall grow.
> A twig shall sprout.
> The spirit of the Lord shall alight upon this child.
> A spirit of wisdom and insight,
> A spirit of counsel and valor,
> A spirit of devotion and reverence.
> They shall sense the truth,
> Shall judge the poor with equity
> And decide with justice for the lowly of the land.
> Justice and faithfulness shall be theirs.
> The wolf shall dwell with the lamb,
> The leopard lie down with the kid;
> The calf and the lion together
> And a little child shall lead them.

Rabbi Reflections:

(The Rabbi who officiates at the ceremony will be asked to offer a reflection. To show as example, the following is a transcript of a sermon given during the holy season of Hanukkah, 2003 by Rabbi Misha Tillman of Chicago.)

"And a little child shall lead them. It is a very important reference in the Bible --- the importance of a child in the ideal picture of the world, if you will. We are at that time of year, the winter holidays, when we are about to celebrate Hanukkah, when many of us are preparing to celebrate Christmas and of course when we will celebrate our patriotic duty to shop! So it is that time of year, that those that own businesses get business; often, the rich get richer. And those who are not rich, they still shop, they still spend money, they put it on the credit card so the poor get poorer. It is a time of exaggeration---of largess, of things and experiences heightened. And so, my friends, unfortunately the winter holidays have become so commercialized. Yet let us forget the external, but concentrate on the spiritual dimensions of the holiday, for it is there we find the sacred, it is where we find the emphatic affirmation of the importance of family, the importance of children in our lives. Hanukkah, like many Jewish holidays, is a holiday celebrated at home. But think about it---out of all Christian holidays, Christmas is probably the one that also is celebrated at home (while certainly we begin in the church with a more public celebration). So this is the time of the year when the concept of family is very strong in our minds and in our hearts. Hanukkah is the holiday known as 'the festival of the lights'; on Hanukkah we light the menorah as you all know, or in Hebrew the 'Hanukkia'. Each night we light an additional candle in the celebration. In fact, it was taught that Adam was able to contemplate the divine light for 36 hours, the divine light having been created on the first day, before it was hidden – therefore on Hanukkah we light 36 candles. Where do we place the menorah? We place it in the most visible place in our homes so that everyone can see it; we place it between us and other people to see. For the light represents the Divine presence; the Divine presence first and foremost is not just in heaven – it is not even within our hearts: it is first and foremost between people, between human beings, in human relationship. And what relationship is more sacred, more intimate than between a parent and a child?

So at this sacred time, when we celebrate in the spirit of two great traditions the bestowal of Hebrew Names and the Baptism of this child, we also wish that the Divine Light should always shine brightly between ourselves and our children, and that there would always be a sanctity, a sense of the sacred, in our relationship with them, for they are our future. They are those that will continue the infinite chain of generations of our two great traditions. So may the light of these holidays shine brightly not only from heaven, not only in our hearts, but also between all of us. Amen."

THE SECOND READER COMES FORTH FROM THE GATHERING

Second Reading: 1 John 4:7-12

> Beloved, let us love one another because love is of God; for everyone who loves is begotten of God and has knowledge of God. The person without love has known nothing of God, for God is love. Love, then consists in this: not that we have loved God, but that God has loved us. Beloved, if God has loved us so, we must have the same love for one another. No one has ever seen God. Yet if we love one another, God dwells in us, and God's love is brought to perfection in us.

Priest Reflection:

(The priest next steps forward to offer a reflection on the text and the celebration of Baptism. What follows here is a transcript of the sermon spoken during the Christmas season, 2003 by Rev. Jerry Jacobs of Arlington Heights, Chicago.)

"Calling someone beloved intimates a very significant relationship; it is someone we would do anything for. We would lay down our life to our beloved. That's the depth of a love that our faith tradition calls us to, to many extents. In our lives, especially given the events of September 11, 2001, I think we are so much more aware, so much more conscious of--while people call God by many different names--true authentic faith in a God that is a loving God, a creating God, works for the good of all. It is not a God that puts walls and divisions up and says 'you believe this and you believe that, and so you are not in our group; therefore, we will push you away'. True faith in any true faith community that is authentic is about bringing people together in peaceful ways, to live a good life. You are holding your beloved children right now, children that you would do anything for. Your greatest hopes and dreams for these children is that they will grow up to realize God's plans for their lives: that they will embody the best of their parents and grandparents, the best of their godparents, the best of their aunts and uncles, that somehow those things that you most value, the traditions and customs this child will learn, to understand why they are important. This is why we do this ceremony between Jews and Christians, so that we as Christians learn that we are rooted in Judaism, we are so interconnected. We as Christians owe everything to Judaism. Our whole faith is based on Jesus, who was Jewish! And all that He believed was based on Torah. So if we are authentic Christians, we have profound respect and admiration for people of the Jewish faith. That is what we are called for, and what this ritual today embodies in so many ways. And so as we go through the rest of this ritual today, we are aware that rituals are wonderful in that they point to God. No words can ever fully explain who God is! God breaks into the world in so many different ways, and so our symbols of lighting candles for example ---whether it be a Hanukkah candle or a light on an advent wreath, candles being the sign of hope, that God breaks into our world and breaks into our lives. There is a quote, attributed to St. Thomas Aquinas, saying 'every time a child is born is a sign from God that the world is to go on.' So we live as hopeful people, hopeful that these children will be a light for us as they lead us in ways of love, ways of holiness. Amen."

COMMITMENT TO A FAITH FILLED LIFE

Rabbi: Since all of us make up the family of God's people and have committed ourselves to share the very best of our faith and traditions with these children, let us join together in recommitting ourselves to a faith filled life.

Priest: We believe that where people are gathered together in love, God is present and good things happen and life is rich and full. We believe that we are immersed in mystery, and that our lives are more than they seem. We belong to each other and to a universe of great creative energies whose source and destiny is God. We believe that the Spirit of peace is present with us as God's people, as we celebrate our common existence and the fidelity of God. And most deeply, we believe that in our struggle to love, we Incarnate God in the world. And so, aware of mystery and wonder, caught in friendship and laughter, we celebrate the sacredness of life in our gathering today. Amen.

THE BAPTISM WITH WATER

(At this time, families with their children and godparents proceed one at a time, upon being called, to the pool or font for the pouring of water. Whether the child is immersed in the pool, or water poured over them, the words spoken are the same that is using the Trinitarian formula.)

Priest: Humankind has always perceived both the life-giving and death-dealing nature of water. In the stories of creation and of the great flood, we see water as a symbol of life and death. Israel was led out of slavery through the Red Sea to be an image of God's holy people. Jesus walked into the waters of the Jordan and emerged anointed with the Spirit.

     And so parents, I ask you: is it your will that your child be baptized in the faith of God's people which we have professed with you?

Parents: Yes, it is.

(as water is poured over the head of the child)

Priest: I baptize you (*the baby's name*) this day in God's name. In the name of the Father, and of the Son, and of the Holy Spirit. Amen.

     Let us rejoice in the gift of new life!

All Gathered: Blessed be God forever, for God has blessed and chosen these children, as God's very own.

ANOINTING WITH OIL

(Within Catholic tradition, the use of oil is coupled with the motif of being priest, prophet and king: the priest representative of one who reminds us of all that is holy in our lives; the prophet one who bears the truth, even when it is

difficult to hear; and the king, a reminder to be centered on the welfare of others, by being a responsible leader.[1])

Rabbi: From ancient times, oil has always been a symbol of royalty and nobility. Kings and queens were anointed as a sign of the great dignity of their call to lead and serve their people with love and tenderness. If God is King, as God's children we share a royal dignity. The sweet scent of oil is a reminder of the marvelous gift of human life. We now anoint these children with this precious oil. May it serve as a reminder of the great dignity and nobility of what it means to be a child of the Most High.

Children are anointed.

BLESSINGS OF EARS AND MOUTH

(This ritual comes from the Greek word Ephphetha, which means 'be opened'. This is a beautiful rite that reminds us of the need, especially in contemporary culture, to open our ears to hear and our mouths to speak all that is of God.)

Priest: *(The name of the child)*, you have been given birth and have been welcomed into God's people. May God soon touch your ears that You might hear God's word, and your mouth, that you might proclaim God's praises to all Creation.

BLESSINGS OF THE WINE
(We know that the Talmud tells us that Kiddush was introduced between the 6th and 4th centuries B.C.E. by the Men of the Great Assembly.[2] For this ceremony, the family might use the Kiddush cup from their wedding, or perhaps from their own initiation ceremony as a child.)

Rabbi: The Hebrew word for holy or sanctification is Kiddush. This celebration is a holy and special moment. And so we ask God's blessing on this wine and we toast these children with great joy.

Baruch Atah Adonai Eloheynu Melech Ha-o'lam, Boreh P'ri Hagafen

Blessed are You, O Lord our God, King of the Universe, Who created the fruit of the vine. Amen

(The wine is shared with each child)

PASSING OF THE LIGHT

(Each family is given a small candle at this point. When it is their turn, this small candle will be lit from the Paschal candle, thereby signifying the presence of the light of the Divine within them. It is a reminder to all of their awesome responsibility to keep that light aflame through all time.)

Priest: Parents, you will be the first teachers of your children in the ways of faith, hope and love. You are called to keep the flame of your love burning brightly between you.

A candle is handed to the parents.

      May you share the brightness of God's light and love with your children for many years to come. Amen.

PRAYERS OF PETITION

Priest: We are a people concerned about passing our faith and traditions on to our children. Therefore, let us bring our prayers before God. May all gathered here please respond "God Hear Our Prayer" after each petition.

Parents: That our families may be strengthened in a deeper bond of love, care and unity through our commitment to these children. We pray.....

      That our lives as parents and the lives of our Godparents may be continuing examples of integrity, goodness and justice. We pray....

That our children may know the power and presence of our love, our affection and our tenderness. We pray.....

For a continuing growth in understanding, openness and unity among all people who share faith in God. We pray....

RECEPTION OF THE CHILDREN

Rabbi: Let us now mention our own hopes, dreams and prayers for these children and parents in the silence of our hearts.

(Pause)

O God, these children are truly blessed. Grant their parents and families the strength and conviction necessary to raise them in the very best of our shared traditions of faith. Grant all of us health of body, mind and spirit, that we may enjoy fullness of years and live according to your will in faithfulness. Amen.

All are asked to extinguish their candles.

Priest: As a sign of our common commitment as God's people, I invite the parents, Godparents and all who share the search for faith, to greet these children through a sign of blessing and welcome.

All gathered may bless this child through a touch, a kiss, or any other expression of joy.

CLOSING PRAYERS

Priest: The Our Father is one of the most significant prayers in the Christian tradition. Finding its roots and theme in the Jewish tradition, in turn taught by Jesus to his followers, it calls upon our God in great trust and confidence. Let us join together as we pray:

Our Father, who art in heaven, hallowed be Thy name. Thy kingdom come, Thy will be done on earth, as it is in heaven. Give us this day our daily bread, and forgive us our trespasses, as we forgive those who trespass against us. And lead us not into temptation, but deliver us from evil. For Thine is the kingdom and the power and the glory, now and forever. Amen.

Rabbi:

The Sh'ma has always been the most important statement of faith in the Jewish tradition. Today, we are emphasizing a great deal not only of similarity, but also true congeniality between two great religious traditions. We recognize that when Jesus was asked by his disciples to teach them how to pray, he shared with them the Sh'ma. Therefore I invite everyone to share with each other this great prayer, the Sh'ma, taken from the Book of Deuteronomy.

Sh'ma Yisrael Adonai Eloheynu Adonai Echad
Hear O Israel, You are of God and God is One.

Baruch Shem K'vod Malchuto L'olam Va-ed.
Praise be the Presence of God's Glorious Kingdom Forever

FINAL BENEDICTION

(The service concludes with this very important blessing. In ancient Israel, the priests that served in the Temple in Jerusalem were instructed to bless the assembled congregation with a special blessing, known as Birkat Kohanim, the Priestly Benediction. It is found in the Book of Numbers, chapter 6, verses 24-26.)

Rabbi: Yivarechecha Adonai Ve-Yishmerecha

Priest: May the Lord bless you and keep you.

Rabbi: Yaer Adonai Panav Elecha Vi-Hunecha

Priest: May the Lord cause His face to shine upon you and be gracious to you.

Rabbi: *Yisa Adonai Panav Elecha Ve-Yasem Lecha Shalom*

Priest: May the Lord lift His countenance toward you and give you peace.

Let us offer a sign of our affirmation and congratulations and support for these children and parents

(applause – applause)

ENDNOTES

1. *Infant Baptism, A Sourcebook for Parishes* (Catholic Bishop of Chicago, 2001) p.3-26

2. See Alfred J. Kolatch, *The Jewish Book of Why* (New York: Jonathan David Publishers, 1981) p. 172

Ceremony Check List

✓ Ceremonial Program Book

✓ Facilitator/Mentor

✓ Baptismal Candles

✓ Matches

✓ Towels to Dry the Child

✓ Container of Chrism

✓ Microphone

✓ Baptism Registration Forms

✓ Readers

✓ Copy of Text for Readers

✓ Godparents

✓ Hebrew Names (and meanings) Chosen

✓ Program, with Hebrew names of the children, their parents and Godparents

✓ Musicians

✓ Water

✓ Pitcher

✓ Fees to Clergy

Commonly Asked Questions, or "Gee, I Didn't Know That!"

Often we assume that we still know the answers to questions long forgotten, or in fact, never fully understood in the first place. In some instances, information and our understanding of theology have changed from when we learned our lessons as children. What follows is a brief overview of questions that often occur in interfaith partnerships, especially when considering formal sacramental preparation.

1. What is the current teaching regarding Original Sin?

The concept of original sin was refined in the deliberations of the Council of Trent (1545-1563), though nuanced first from Old Testamentscriptures (the fall of man in chapter three of Genesis), then broadened by the writings of St. Paul in his letter to the Romans (we are told by author Raymond Brown, S.S., Ph.D., that "Romans has been the most studied of the apostles' writings...from Augustine through Abelard, Luther and Calvin to Barth, this letter has played a major role in the development of theology."[1]).

So knowing the complexity of these writings and with just a cursory view of the text, we read from St. Paul

> *"Therefore, just as through one person sin entered the world, and through sin death , and thus death came to all, inasmuch as all sinned (Rom 5:12)...For just as through the disobedience of one person the many were made sinners, so through the obedience of one the many will be made righteous." (Rom 5:19)*

Simply put, recent biblical scholarship has taught us it was Paul's understanding that it was the "virus of sin" that invaded humanity; that there was now in the world a ghastly power which impeded the Almighty's vision.

In the fourth century, St. Augustine began to expound his theories condemning the innocent unbaptized children. In an earlier setting, Augustine took a softer approach, stating in *De libero arbitrio III*: "It is superfluous to inquire about the merits of one who has not any merits. For one need not hesitate to hold that life may be neutral as between good conduct and sin, and that as between reward and punishment there may be a neutral sentence of the judge." A few years later, after doing theological battle with a group of heretics (called Pelagians) over this issue, Augustine embraced a harsher tone in support of those unbaptised children being banished to misery and fiery damnation, declaring

> *"Those unfortunate children who die without baptism must face the judgment of God. They are vessels of contumely, vessels of wrath and the wrath of God is upon them."[2]*

WHEW! It wasn't until centuries later that church theologians broke with Augustinian thought to adopt a gentler, more straightforward understanding of original sin.

In modern times, we have come to discern that original sin is not meant to be understood as a *personal* sin in Catholic theology. A current understanding is this: each one of us is born into a world that is  broken. Evil exists. We all understand the story of Adam and Eve in the Hebrew Scriptures and how, when given Paradise they couldn't handle it. They messed it up! So the world that was paradise and one of perfect love was changed: changed to a world of brokenness, sickness and death. The original blessing of God in creation, that "this world is good", was changed by humankind's free choice.

Father Richard Gula, S.S., writing in *Catholic Update*, tells us original sin "is a condition of being human that makes us feel as if our freedom were bound by chains from the very beginning. We feel the effects of this evil in the pull towards selfishness, which alienates us from our deeper selves, from others and from God. Because of original sin, we will always know struggle and tragedy as part of our life….In order to rise above the power of evil, we need to open ourselves to the presence of…love. This love comes to us through others witnessing to justice, truth and peace."[3] Through Baptism, one is initiated into a larger community, the church. This is the community of people who hold these values and this way of seeing and loving and serving one another to mend the part of the world that is so broken.

In his book "Biblical Literacy", Rabbi Joseph Teluskin explains that while the concept of original sin is significant in Christian theology, it does not occupy such importance within Jewish thinking. In fact, the predominant view among Jewish scholars is "people sin *as* Adam and Eve sinned, not *because* they sinned."[4] For a different view, Rabbi Lawrence Kushner offers a midrashic explanation for Adam and Eve's expulsion from the Garden of Eden. His explanation has more to do with a child's pain associated with leaving home in their struggle to become autonomous humans than with sin. He envisions a conversation between Adam and Eve and God, with the couple declaring their longing for long walks together in the garden "just like when we were little." "I am truly sorry," states God, "but as every adult knows, no matter how graceful, every 'growing up' necessitates life-long pain. And that hurt, at the core of our soul, is what renders normal people, on rare occasions, capable of great evil. People hurt others because they were hurt. And they were hurt because that is the price of adulthood – there is no other way."[5] Simply, he states, Adam and Eve were set up--not by the snake, but by God! There was no sin – this was what was supposed to happen, for "children disobey their parents and in doing so, complete their own creation."[6]

2.   Who can baptize?

The usual ministers of Baptism are the Bishop, or a priest. However, in emergency or necessary circumstances, anyone can baptize, as long as the intent is clear (that is, the intention is that of the church) and the proper Trinitarian wording is used.

Keep in mind, the key to these sacramental moments is *relationship*. We don't want our clergy to be "hired guns", people we can count on to punch our card as we move lockstep through life and the faith lives of our families. Clergy can be an important bridge to the faith of a community: meet them, know them, interact with them before your ceremony. Don't be a stranger to the community as you stand before them with your child: be in relationship with them!

3. *If my baby was baptized in the bathtub, do I need to have it "re-done" by a Priest?*

Given the intrinsic nature of the sacrament, once the baby (or person for that matter) has been consecrated by the pouring of water and the proper words issued saying 'I baptize you in the Name of the Father, and of the Son, and of the Holy Spirit", the Baptism is complete and authentic. In fact, once given, it cannot be repeated. Of course, this is not the preferred manner of Baptism and should be avoided unless absolutely necessary!

4. *If faith is a journey, why baptize children at all? Why not wait till they are adults and have an understanding of God's love in a personal way?*

As we know, it has long been the practice of the church to baptize infants. Although early church leaders only baptized adults, when Christianity became the religion of Rome (in the beginning of the fourth century) it became the tradition to baptize whole families: adults, children and infants alike. Some scholars believe that the rite of infant baptism grew out of the need to administer to those sick and dying; and over time, this case became the norm. For the first time, the church acknowledged the person to be baptized was not an adult, and that while the infant would not be able to  speak for themselves, it was the faith of the "church" that would instruct, sustain and guide them as they grew. It is to this point that we return to the original question. Baptism is but the threshold of a spiritual beginning, with the emphasis being on the **foundation**: faith **is** a journey to discover the truth of God's love for us. (It should be noted due to the remarkable reforms undertaken by the Second Vatican Council in the early 1960's, two separate rites of initiation were developed, one for adults and one for infants, thereby acknowledging the special needs of each population.[7])

As partners in an interfaith relationship, we are given an exquisite opportunity to come to this moment as spiritually grounded **adults**, prepared to honor the commitments made. As we make adult decisions, there are considerations as we move to those rites of passage that concern our children:

- Why do I want my child to participate in this rite of passage? Am I only trying to recreate my own experience? Or does our participation reflect our new family's spiritual activity?

- Have I considered my partner's desires? How is he/she feeling: excluded? A sense of loss? Are they mourning? Left out? Losing out?

- Are we participating in this ritual just to please our parents?

- Are we participating in this ritual merely because the "calendar" tells us to do so?

- Do we want to oblige a social obligation?

- Am I practicing my own religious traditions? If I'm not, why do I feel the need to have my children do so? Is this the moment to help me reconnect to those traditions?

Mary Rosenbaum, director of the Dovetail Institute for Interfaith Family Resources and author of *Celebrating Our Differences*, is a Catholic woman married to a Jewish man for 36 years and mother of three grown children, none of whom are practicing Christians. In a recent conversation she was asked whether she would raise her children differently if given the opportunity. She responded in this way, saying: "One of the things I would do differently is having them baptized as infants. If I were starting out today I don't think I would do that, and I don't think the Church would let me. They put a greater emphasis today on there being a reasonable expectation that this infant will ratify the decision, the covenant, implied by Baptism. When our kids were born, it seemed more like getting your hand stamped at the prom ---a sort of sign of entry. Now they (the church) want a greater commitment that you're actually going

When our kids were born, it seemed more like getting your hand stamped at the prom --- a sort of sign of entry. Now they (the church) want a greater commitment that you're actually going to produce a Catholic adult, and I think they're right about that.

to produce a Catholic adult, and I think they are right about that. It would have been better for us to hold off, I think now..."[8]

It is critically important that we come to this moment as authentic, confident people. Just as you have given tremendous thought to the care of your child (whether it be what you will feed them, the house they will live in, they schools they will attend), parents should take care not to impose an artificial identity on their children, but come to this moment with great care, thought and conversation with your partner.

5. What is limbo and do Christians still believe in it?

It might be said upfront that no Pope in history has mandated limbo as dogma. It was simply a construct, that is, a creation of the church to assist in clarifying a prickly dilemma created by the doctrine of original sin.

That being said, the concept of limbo, derived from the word *limbus* (Late Latin deriv.) and meaning "on the border" or "edge" arose as a response by church fathers to the question of what happens to two distinct and separate populations at their death.

The first population concerned the souls of those infants who die prior to being baptized. While it seemed harsh to consign those poor souls to hell, through no fault of their own, it was a contradiction of basic Christian theology of salvation through a water rebirth. In response to this dilemma, the church fashioned the theory of *limbus infantum*, a place for those babies to wait to be escorted into heaven. The current status of limbo and the question of "what happens?" to those unbaptized children at death has been clarified somewhat by the recent Vatican document, *Gaudium et Spes* 22. It says "For since Christ died for all (Rom. 8:32)...we must hold that the Holy Spirit offers to all the possibility of being made partners, in a way known to God, in the paschal mystery."[9] Put simply, the church chooses not to speculate about those who die unbaptized.

> The key in choosing a godparent is that they be someone with a deep religious commitment rather than just someone who is a family member or friend.

The second population in question was those holy men and women who died before the time of Jesus Christ, such as Abraham. Where did their souls languish? The answer created by the church was *limbus patrum,* a temporary state (albeit) of happiness somewhere between purgatory and heaven. Of course, once Christ ascended into heaven, all those bound there were let loose to share in the glories of God's eternal kingdom.[10]

6.   *Where did the tradition of Godparents come from, and are they still required today? Do Jews have Godparents?*

When a child is born, families understand the basic obligation they have to provide for their baby the love it craves and the physical attention it needs. They also recognize the obligation they have to provide the moral guidance their child needs to have; in fact, they often know there is no more important role in life than "growing a child" into adulthood.

It is the task then of the godparent to support the child as he (she) grows into faith. From the beginning of the third century, at the time of infant baptism, parents pledged to teach their children the Lord's Prayer, the Ten Commandments and the Apostles Creed. However, with persecution widespread at that time, there was no guarantee that the parents would survive to fulfill their promise. So came the role of the godparent: one chosen to embrace the mission of the parent---that is, to raise the child as a Christian.

In modern times, we look to the current *Catechism of the Catholic Church* for a formal understanding of the role of godparents:

> *For the grace of Baptism to unfold, the parents' help is important. So too is the role of **godfather and godmother,** who must be firm believers, able and ready to help the newly baptized – child or adult – on the road to Christian life. Their task is a truly ecclesial function.... (1255)*

While the key in choosing a godparent is that they be someone with a deep religious commitment rather than just someone who is a family member or friend, there are other specific guidelines to follow[11]:

- They must be sixteen years old;

- They must be a Catholic who has been baptized, received Communion and has been confirmed;

- They must not be the child's parents;

- There must be at least <u>one</u> godparent who is a Catholic in "good standing" (that is, someone who attends Mass and who, if married, is in a valid marriage.)

In addition to the above-mentioned requirements, there are a few other things to know as you choose a godparent:[12]

- Technically, a person who is not Catholic is unable to serve as a godparent (given the requirements as stated above). However, as only one Catholic godparent is required, it is customary in a Catholic Jewish family to honor a Jewish individual and invite them to serve as a "witness." This person then is invited to participate in the entire ceremony, whose name will be entered into the register as such, alongside that of the godparent (the  reason being, of course, is that the obligation to be godparent is not merely a friend who will encourage good behavior, albeit Christian, but rather someone who will step forward and represent the community into which the child is being baptized. The godparent then is obligated to "stand-in" for the parent if they were unable to provide for the child's religious training.)

- Sometimes a family will choose a person to be godparent who, for some reason, is unable to attend the ceremony. In this case, a "proxy" may be chosen to represent this individual.

- It is recommended that if two godparents are chosen, they be of different genders. If only one is chosen, they need not be the same sex as the child.

- Regarding the choice of a Baptismal name, again the Catechism tells us that *"parents, sponsors and the pastor are to see that a name is not given that is foreign to Christian sentiment."* (CCC 1256.)

7.   *What is a Sandek? Is it the same thing as being a Godparent in the Jewish tradition?*

There are no godparents in Judaism; unlike Christianity, the responsibility of the religious upbringing of the child lies solely with the parents.

It is an honor to be the sandek, the male person who holds the baby on a pillow, which is then placed on his lap, during the ceremony of *brit milah* (which was discussed in the previous chapter.) This is purely a meritorious act, usually given to the grandfather. The sandek, also called *tofes ha-yeled* the "holder of the child" or *av sheni* the "second father"[13], is the one who physically presents the child as he is welcomed into the Abrahamic covenant with God. The empty chair of Elijah is usually placed next to the chair of the sandek.

8.   *I would prefer to have this ceremony in private, perhaps in my home. Is this possible? I am worried about the reaction of my Jewish parents, who have never been in a church.*

The traditional location for the celebration of Baptism is a church; a Naming ceremony can take place either at home or at the synagogue. The key, however, is to be surrounded by a *community* of people, a gathering of those who will support, nurture and guide your child, with you. The very nature of Baptism, that it is representative of the faith of a people, is contrary to the ceremony being celebrated in isolation. While some might feel *their* child will be lost in the celebration where many babies are present, great care is given to name, bless and honor each child individually.

It is important that you understand your desire to have a ceremony in private. Sometimes, given the nature of the dynamics between parents and grandparents when it comes to child-rearing, we strive to keep harmony at all costs. Stories are plentiful where Jewish grandparents blanch (and worse) at the thought of their grandchild being baptized, and Catholic grandparents are vocal in expressing their dismay at a change from the ceremony they cherish. Advice abounds regarding the role grandparents play in helping to raise children born of an interfaith union, and the difficulties therein. Therapist Barbara Rudnick, of the Jewish Family and Children's Service in Minneapolis, says she receives many calls each year from Jewish grandparents seeking ways to force their children to raise their interfaith grandchildren as Jews. "What's key," she says, "is keeping the relationship alive: it's not about making somebody do something the way you want them to, it's about respecting adult children making choices that make sense for their lives. Of course, supporting those choices even when you don't approve of them is tricky!"[14] Rabbi and therapist Arthur Blecher says: "Their (the grandparents) primary concern is not the happiness of their son or daughter, but whether they as individuals will bond or identify with the grandchildren, particularly if the grandchildren are raised in a different religion. They don't come in stating this as their primary concern, but it emerges pretty fast that they're really worried that they're not going to fit in, that they'll feel alienated from their grandchildren."[15] Author and therapist Sam Osherson, writing for the Jewish Outreach Institute, adds, "As a grown son or daughter, it can help to realize that your parents are struggling with worries and anxieties of their own. They may need your calm reassurance and help in not burning any bridges...on the other hand, you should not feel completely responsible for a parent's reactions. You can't ultimately control their responses. Better to be as clear and direct and loving as possible, but not expect that if you only did it right they would not respond negatively."[16]

The thought of these ceremonies can be very threatening to grandparents: ultimately, time, understanding, information and love will help surmount their fears. What is essential is that there be **honest, open** and **respectful** communication between the parents of the baby. If you still have questions, you need to find the answers; if there are things you don't understand, you need to be re-educated. Once you are unified as a couple, the concerns, questions and fears of grandparents and others are easier to respond to with courage, calm and compassion. Undoubtedly, their role as grandparents will remain an authentic one, however, one

Parents need to be secure and confident in the steps they are taking to begin their journey of faith *as a family*, before they can be able to explain their desires to others.

which belongs solely to them: that of being a role model to their grandchildren as they express the tenets and rituals of their faith traditions. One suggested resource both for you and for your parents is *Mingled Roots: A Guide for Jewish Grandparents of Interfaith Grandchildren* by Sunie Levin (published by B'nai B'rith Women, 1991). Simply written, this book offers grandparents specific, concrete things to do for and with your grandchildren.

9. *While my husband is Jewish, I am Catholic. Will my baby be considered Jewish?*

In Jewish law, the matters of one's personal status are quite interesting. The traditional Jewish approach is that if one is born of a Jewish mother, then one is a Jew. It is important to note that in Judaism one cannot stop being a Jew. An individual born of a Jewish mother will be a Jew even if raised/converted in/to another religion. Consideration must be given to the case of the person whose only Jewish parent is the father. In traditional Jewish law, this person is not considered to be a Jew. However, in 1983, the Reform movement in the United States ruled that those individuals whose father is Jewish, but whose mother is not are still considered to be Jews if raised in a Jewish home. This led to quite a controversy in the Jewish community throughout the world. Needless to say, the Orthodox and Conservative movements categorically rejected this approach! Reform movements outside of the US were a bit reserved in their reaction as well. Many reform rabbis to this day do not follow the 1983 ruling: while their hearts and minds may agree, congregation life forces them to abide by the ruling.

In reality, the 1983 ruling in question is a reflection of a massive trend in American Jewish life, which reform leaders acknowledge. Because the Reform movement makes up the lion's share of affiliated American Jews, it is easy to guess that it is only a matter of time before the issue of patrilineality will be adopted in one form or another in the entire Jewish community in the USA.

10. *How can children be both Catholic and Jewish if they are baptized? Don't they cancel each other out?*

This is probably the toughest question facing new parents when confronting this rite of passage, and I must preface my comments by acknowledging that my answer is probably not the one you would hear from your parish priest, nor rabbi.

That being said, here is my understanding of the experience: Baptism is an orientation towards God. It is the confirmation of the belief of the parent and that of their religious community, the church. It is a symbol of inclusion, rather than exclusion, whereby you are recognized as the beloved child of God. You are invited to participate in God's unfathomable grace, through the embrace of the community at large. Baptism is a transitional moment in time: emerging from the waters, one is given the choice to live a life of Love, as directed and embodied by Christ, or not. As the parents (with the support of the godparents) speak for the child, it becomes **their challenge and responsibility** to act accordingly and honor the commitment to the "Amen" they speak. Years later, it is at the moment of confirmation as a young adult that your child will choose to echo those promises that were made <u>for</u> them years earlier.

In my mind, Catholic and Jewish don't "cancel each other out." They celebrate the bounty of God's love for us, using the language of both of our religious traditions. Just as by Naming we become relational with God, it is through Baptism that we are claimed by God as belonging to Him.

That is how I understand things to be. However, for another perspective, keep reading! What follows next is the vision of a rabbi and a priest, in conversation.

ENDNOTES

1. See author and theologian Rev. Raymond E. Brown, *An Introduction to the New Testament* (New York: Doubleday, 1997) p. 559

2. Author Charles Panati writing in *Sacred Origins of Profound Things* (New York: Arkana, 1996) p. 489 details the historical framework of the writings of Augustine in the fourth century and the theology stemming therein. For additional resources regarding original sin, please see *The Catholic Encyclopedia, Volume XI*, Copyright 1911, and the online version found at newadvent.org.

3. Rev. Richard Gula, S.S., writing in the journal <u>Catholic Update,</u> January 1997.

4. See Rabbi Joseph Teluskin, *Biblical Literacy* (New York: William Morrow & Co., 1997) p.10

5. Rabbi Lawrence Kushner, *God was in this Place and I, I did not know* (Woodstock, Vt: Jewish Lights Publishing, 1991) p. 74

6. *Ibid.,* p. 75

7. For information regarding specific rites of baptism, please see *Christian Initiation,* "General Introduction," (Revised, 1983); *Rite of Christian Initiation o f Adults* (1974, English 1988); and *Rite of Baptism for Children* (1969) all of which may be found in *The Rites of the Catholic Church, Vol. I,* Collegeville, Minnesota: The Liturgical Pres, 1990.

8. These comments originate from a panel discussion on "Daily Life in Interfaith Families" during the *Dovetail Institute' s* Conference, June 2000. The speaker is Mary Helen Rosenbaum,, Editor of *Dovetail Magazine.* For more information on the complete transcript, see issue T11:00.

9. Quoted from The Catholic FAQ at newadvent.org, *Gaudium et spes* (December 7, 1965) and found in the *Catechism of the Catholic Church* 1260.

10. Charles Panati, ibid., p. 487

11. See Paul Turner, *Your Child's Baptism* (Chicago: Liturgy Training Publication, 1999) p. 8-9

12. *Ibid.,* p.10-11

13. The translation offered by Dr. Rachel Dulin, Ph.D., Professor of Bible at Spertus Institute, Chicago, Illinois.

14. These comments originate from a panel discussion entitled "How Do We Spoil Them? Grandparenting in Interfaith Families" held at the *Dovetail Institute* Conference June 2000. For a complete transcript, please see issue T:16:00

15. These comments originate from Rabbi Dr. Arthur Bleicher's presentation at the June 2000 *Dovetail Institute* Conference, and re-printed in *Dovetail Magazine* (T5:00).

16. Rabbi Sam Osherson, "Grandparents: The Hidden Link in Interfaith Marriages", written in the internet newsmagazine

InterfaithFamily.com, August 15, 2002 in an issue devoted to the topic of Grandparents.

A Conversation Between Clergy:
A Lesson in Dialogue

What follows is a conversation between a Catholic Priest, Rev. Bernie Pietrzak, and a Reform Rabbi, Misha Tillman, which was recorded in August 2003 in Mt. Prospect, Illinois. After a brief introduction, these gentlemen address questions concerning Jewish and Catholic rites of passage and how they complement--or contradict--one another.

❋ ❋ ❋ ❋ ❋

FATHER BERNIE PIETRZAK: My name is Father Bernie Pietrzak and I'm a priest from the Archdiocese of Chicago. I've been working with the Jewish-Catholic Couples Dialogue Group now for about 10 to 12 years. A fellow priest invited me to be part of the group when I was working in Deerfield, Illinois, a community which is about 45 percent Jewish. I became more and more a part of the group by co-officiating weddings with the Rabbis in town and as time went on, supporting these same couples as they had children. This emerging group of families tried to find creative ways, ways with integrity, to celebrate the birth of their children, and I was asked to participate in these initiation rites. For the last four or five years, we have celebrated close to 30 to 40 baby naming christenings per year; that is, the shared service officiated by a Rabbi and a Priest where couples celebrate the fullness of both of their traditions as they welcome their children into their families.

RABBI MISHA TILLMAN: I'm Rabbi Michael Tillman; I'm also known as Misha Tillman. I have been involved with the group for about five, six years now, and it has become a very important part of my rabbinical work. As I have become more involved with the group, I have come to realize how critically important things that are happening in this group are. Particularly, because the group itself is a grassroots movement. It is very important that the group is not affiliated formally with any organization: this means that it reflects not somebody's agenda, but a true spiritual need, a need that we are trying to address the best we possibly can. As far as the baby-naming and baptism ceremony is concerned, it really has become the next logical step for those families that have celebrated their marriages by continuing to honor their respective traditions as they have children and start their education and upbringing.

MS SMITH: Thank you both. Question Number One: Father Bernie, you might comment on this. Why do you need to be baptized to say you're a member of the Catholic Church?

FATHER BERNIE PIETRZAK: As Catholics, we have a very strong sacramental tradition. In other words, what that means is that we believe that there are these heightened moments of encounter with God in life. In the sacramental moments of life, these are especially significant encounters with God, where God is very present to the moment, to the situation. We also are able to be more receptive and aware of this presence of God in these moments. Baptism is probably the most important sacrament of our tradition. It names who we are, who we follow, the dying and rising of Christ we participate in. It's the beginning, the initiation sacrament. It's not so much about jumping through hoops as the question seems to indicate, it's saying -- this is the beginning of a relationship with God that is informed by Jesus Christ. Obviously there are a variety of ways that people come to follow God in the diverse society and world that we live in, but for Catholics, the person of Jesus Christ is what offers us a path of how we come to know and experience God and what God calls and asks of us in the way we live our lives. It really is a statement of saying that yes, I'm beginning this relationship with Jesus Christ in baptism. Simply, this encounter is the beginning experience for a child or an adult as they receive the water or are baptized in the water of baptism.

RABBI MISHA TILLMAN: Obviously Father Bernie is a much more enlightened expert in the matters of baptism, but as an outsider of the Catholic Church and Christian religion in general, I would like to draw attention to one very important thing that people don't appreciate about Christianity. Christianity is the only religion I can think of into which one cannot be born. You can be born a Jew, as long as your mother is Jewish. A Muslim is anyone who is born of a Muslim father. A Hindu is anyone who is born of a Hindu father. A Zoroastrian is anyone who is born of a Zoroastrian father. Christianity is the only religion into which you cannot be born, which requires you to make that step, either in infancy or in adulthood --

FATHER BERNIE PIETRZAK: Or parents making that step for them.

RABBI MISHA TILLMAN: -- or parents making that step for you, and that is the uniqueness of the Christian tradition. This I think highlights what Father Bernie said: it's not so much jumping through hoops, it's the reflection of the unique Christian spiritual experience. It is a step that a human being has to make or parents of this human being have to make. You cannot just be a Christian, you have to become a Christian, and that's a big difference and that's a uniqueness of Christianity, and I think that's certainly worth noting.

MS. SMITH: When I talk to couples about this combination ceremony, they comment on what appears to them to be an imbalance when comparing baptism and naming. Can you comment on that?

RABBI MISHA TILLMAN: Well, that's connected to what I've just said. One can only become a Christian, and that's what baptism is: becoming a Christian. One can become a Jew, of course, it is possible, but obviously a more common way is being born a Jew. A bris in itself--or the ritual circumcision, for those who are not familiar with the terminology--does not make a person Jewish. It only reaffirms that this person is a part of the Covenant. The traditional, Orthodox Jewish law says as long as one is born of a Jewish mother, one is a Jew, circumcised or not. Of course, in more liberal Jewish circles, if the father is Jewish and the mother is not, the child is also accepted as a Jew very often. The reason, the perception there is some kind of an imbalance has nothing to do with one parent being honored more than the other, one tradition being honored more than the other. It has everything to do with it's just a different way of being a Jew and being a Christian.

During the bris, the child is named; a baby girl is often named 30 days after her birth. Naming of the child is not changing the status of the child from a non-Jew to a Jew. Rather, naming is connecting this child with the Jewish past, with the tradition and with God. The first thing about naming to remember is that if you look at the Bible you will see that all throughout the text of the Torah, people's names change after their encounter with God. Abram became Abraham, Sarai became Sarah and Jacob became Israel: the encounter with the Divine obviously affects deeply and changes entirely the human being. That's the number one reason why we give one a Hebrew name: to connect this person with the Divine. Number two is to establish a connection for this person with the Jewish tradition, with the past, as one other way of connecting with the previous generation of our people. That is why the child is named to honor somebody, whether it is in honor of a deceased relative or some relative that is living: to provide that historical connection. And then third, of course, is what the name does: to accentuate those particular values that the parents want to instill upon this child. For example, Samuel was a prophet who was, as a child, dedicated to the service of God. Those are the things that naming does, but most importantly, it does not change the status of a person, the status of a child.

FATHER BERNIE PIETRZAK: I understand what's important regarding the naming of the child: connecting with the Divine, connecting with God and with the tradition, but also connecting this child with the people of faith, the people of God. If you look at baptism, in many ways, that's exactly the equivalent. I think baptism seems to have a higher power in some people's minds because for so many years it was associated with the idea that if something ever were to happen with this child and this child would die, this child would never come to see God. This child would live in Limbo. The myth of Limbo did exist in our tradition, and I think it heightened baptism's power sometimes for the wrong reasons--out of fear.

RABBI MISHA TILLMAN: Of course, later, one can convert to Judaism. An infant can be converted, so that is possible; but, of course, generally speaking, the way things are, one is born of the

Jewish religion, whereas one cannot be, to be Christian. Probably the more profound truth is what Father Bernie has emphasized, and that truly both of these rituals, baptism and naming, provide this connection with the Divine, the connection with the community and the connection with the family. That's what it does, so in that respect, absolutely, it's an equivalent. The parts are the same thing, they're two sides of the same coin.

MS. SMITH: A Catholic mother has expressed the feeling that the celebration of baptism would be a complete rejection of her Jewish partner. I'd like your thoughts regarding her comment.

RABBI MISHA TILLMAN: If that's how you feel, then yes, it will be a rejection. I think if you perceive an interaction between two spiritual traditions in those terms, rejection versus acceptance, those are extreme terms, those are polar opposites, right? It's white and black, there's not an in-between, there's no gray, then it really will be difficult to develop that relationship further, develop a relationship between two human beings, a Jew and a Catholic. In other words, I think the whole outlook needs a revision here because in reality the relationship, the interaction, is dialogue. It is a mutual education, it is a mutual acceptance to one way or another. Father Bernie has a wonderful line that he continues to use, and that is "in the process (sic: of being in an interfaith marriage) a Jew becomes a little Catholic, and the Catholic becomes a little Jewish", and that's a very wise thing to say. It's not I accept, or reject, it's I learn, I get to know, I explore. And baptism is part of that exploratory form, it's part of that learning, just like the baby naming, and therefore it ought not to be viewed as a rejection of the Jewish partner. Again, you need to look at it, not from the point of view of rejection, but rather from the point of view of mutual enlightenment, at the point of you learning about the child and understanding each other.

FATHER BERNIE PIETRZAK: Regarding this question where it is stated "I feel baptism can be a complete rejection of my Jewish partner", well, does that then mean that before you met your Jewish partner, you were baptized and shared the Eucharist, you were a person of the Catholic tradition so are you rejecting your own Catholicism? You know, when I was in Deerfield in those years, there were a number of times where people in their early 60's would come and talk about how they had converted to Judaism to raise their children. Now that their children were grown they asked --- can I come back to my faith? My experience is that by forcing someone to convert, then it's a lose/lose situation.

RABBI MISHA TILLMAN: I agree --- when it comes to converting, there is always pressure. Then yes, indeed, it is a tug of war. And yes, indeed, there will always be some undercurrents, some suppressed sentiment that something is done at my expense because we committed to raise our child in a way that truly was not mutually agreeable.

FATHER BERNIE PIETRZAK: And there is always a sense of loss, not being able to hand on what I've been raised with or the experience that I had when I was growing up. There's this kind of impetus in parents to want to hand on their experiences to their children not only in religion, but, you know, you look at things like sports, and music. What their children do with that experience is often different. There is a sense of loss when saying, "Okay, we're going to raise our child in only one tradition", as opposed to saying both traditions and have a full sense of a celebration in our house. I think there is a missing piece: the child, as it is becoming an adult, will listen to what God is calling them to throughout their adulthood. This is a very personal thing.

RABBI MISHA TILLMAN: That's right, and I would only add that this experience, Bernie, that you have reflected on is reaping the harvest of what the Jewish Community has been doing for a number of decades. In other words, Reform Judaism adopted the policy that they would look favorably upon, and consider accepting, families and couples where one of them comes from a non-Jewish background, when the non-Jewish spouse converts. In addition, they encourage the couple to make a commitment to create a Jewish home.

See, religion, and religion with which we grew up, provides not necessarily the theological framework of our relationship with God: there's nothing intellectual about our religion. All theology boils down to the same thing. You read Thomas Aquinas, you read Maimonides, they all talk about the same God. The God of the philosophers is the same, but what religion does, is provide an emotional connection, a chain of symbols that we can touch that makes us feel good, that makes us feel worth, that makes us feel connected to the Deity, emotionally. And when the religion with which I grew up is suppressed by way of saying, well, we can't commit to that, we'll have to commit to something else, then that means my emotional life is damaged and I become an incomplete person. It all stays with me as a wound. Secondly, technically speaking, by the Jewish law, any conversion performed for any other reason than the Torah itself is invalid by definition.

In other words, conversion for the sake of marriage is by definition invalid. Nevertheless, with perseverance, deserving a better application, the Jewish establishment--I don't want to be over-critical with the Jewish establishment, but the Jewish establishment pursued that exact line, that exact policy, pressing the non-Jewish partner to convert. In Canada, they follow that very meticulously in fact, and Rabbis are not allowed to officiate at interfaith weddings. They force people to take this course and convert. The thing about it is, not only is it harmful and not only is it generally unsuccessful, but it is simply invalid as far as the Jewish law is concerned. And really, the word rejection here is the last thing that we want to use. The right word to use and the right term to use is again, enlightenment, education, dialogue, and understanding. Well, that's why we're here, to dialogue!

FATHER BERNIE PIETRZAK: And I guess you can turn this question around too. And you could ask the question, I feel that having a bris and having a baby-naming would be a rejection of my Catholic partner, and of course it isn't.

RABBI MISHA TILLMAN: In your eyes it's the same.

FATHER BERNIE PIETRZAK: The wonderful thing in the group (Jewish Catholic Couples Group) is to see more and more couples who aren't engaged yet come into the group before they make a move toward engagement. They're still in the midst of dialoguing about whether or not they have the spaciousness or the openness to accept each other's traditions in a way that's going to be healthy, and helpful, and will call them to a new kind of awareness and growth and understanding of God's presence in their life. I think they also have to recognize that, in a very realistic way, this is a more challenging way of living out your faith. We always try to tell couples that; that it's not for everybody, it's not for everybody --

RABBI MISHA TILLMAN: That's right.

FATHER BERNIE PIETRZAK: -- and it's wise to understand that because if you don't understand that, you're not going to be happy, your spouse is not going to be happy, your children to come are not going to be happy. You're going to create a kind of unspoken subject, a taboo subject and again, if it becomes taboo, then there's a place in that relationship that is not open to dialogue as you say, Misha. And the other thing that I want to say just finally, would be that again, if I love my partner, then I'm going to love everything about them. I'm going to understand and love their flaws and their gifts and their abilities and if they're Jewish or Catholic, I'm going to want to love that and learn more about it. I would think that is what we call people to, or what people call each other to in married life.

Let me just very quickly respond to this. In the last 12 years I've been co-officiating at these weddings; that's about 25 to 30 a year. What I found fascinating is that of those, let's say, 250 weddings that I've been a part of, I have rarely ever experienced such an intolerance from either the Jewish family or the Catholic family. In meeting with couples before the wedding, the experience has often been that the couples ease the fears of their family saying, "I'm not rejecting my Judaism, I'm not rejecting my Catholicism, we're going to try to blend these two traditions together." Once parents understand how their kids are going to approach it, there's a brand new acceptance, it's something new, it's almost exciting, something different. To this day, I've never really experienced some of the prejudice that sometimes we imagine, or hear about. It's probably very real in some settings, but at least to this moment, I've not experienced it.

RABBI MISHA TILLMAN: Yes, I agree; you are right, Bernie. People usually do approach the day of their wedding well prepared. They do discuss this. I remember one couple where I did see intolerance and a lack of being willing to understand. The gentleman was from an Orthodox Jewish background, she was from an extremely conservative Catholic background. After I had met with him, I expressed my doubt. What ended up happening, actually, they did find a priest and they did find another Rabbi. Later on I talked to that priest who was supposed to preside, and this is what he told me. The couple did not show up for the signing of the Ketubah, and when the priest was sent down to check on them, they opened the door and said to the priest, "We're not going to do it." This was one of two times in my life where I said no to the couple, as I just wasn't comfortable doing it. Usually most of the people think this through. You cannot enter a meaningful relationship with somebody of a different religion, without being willing to embrace into another's whole self.

FATHER BERNIE PIETRZAK: Let me make an observation from my experience. I think sometimes this concern shows itself when a couple has been married by a judge --

RABBI MISHA TILLMAN: That's a good observation, yes.

FATHER BERNIE PIETRZAK: -- or a nondenominational minister and so they're facing their blending issues, not at marriage, but they're facing their issues with their kids. But I think they do catch up.

MS. SMITH: I think this question was probably posed by somebody with a six- or seven-year-old, who had not yet dealt with these very original issues.

FATHER BERNIE PIETRZAK: Which goes back to the first question of jumping through hoops!

MS. SMITH: Please comment on this. Catholics say that they're in an interfaith marriage, but they and their relatives are just relieved that the kids have received the sacraments so in fact, they're really Catholic.

RABBI MISHA TILLMAN: Well, I mean, here is the thing.

FATHER BERNIE PIETRZAK: The starting point again.

RABBI MISHA TILLMAN: It's all about the same thing. Wouldn't a Catholic grandmother be happy that her grandchild was baptized? What do you think? I think she would be, and by the same token, wouldn't the Jewish grandmother be happy that her grandchild received a Hebrew baby naming? So it's not about who the child is, where the child stands. The emphasis here is properly put on the process. You can't just be Catholic, you can't just be a Jew, you have to live as a Jew, you have to live as a Catholic.

FATHER BERNIE PIETRZAK: That's right.

RABBI MISHA TILLMAN: And you have to learn! When one party is Jewish and another is Catholic, it's the process of learning, the process of embracing, the process of making steps forward and towards one another. So yes, of course, the Catholic side would be happy, wouldn't they? I submit that the Jewish side also would be happy if the child was in a baby naming ceremony.

FATHER BERNIE PIETRZAK: And let me say this. Again, this has not been my experience. As I listened to the grandparents whose children's wedding I presided at four years earlier, speak at a baby naming Christening moment, they talk with great joy about the fact that their kids are probably more a person of faith now than they would have been had they married one of their own.

RABBI MISHA TILLMAN: Because it's an effort, it's a much larger effort.

FATHER BERNIE PIETRZAK: They put forth more. Oftentimes, when you marry a non-Catholic or non-Jewish person, all of a sudden you have to go back to your own teaching and catechism and relearn it through adult eyes because you have to be able to answer questions that your partner will have. Where if you are marrying a person from the same religious tradition, well, it's presumed, and that dialogue doesn't take place. My experience has been, more often than not, that grandparents have not been so much relieved as much as delighted. They feel their children wouldn't be involved in church or synagogue if they hadn't found each other.

RABBI MISHA TILLMAN: And just to illustrate that point, I often meet with a couple and often the Catholic bride knows more about Jewish customs and traditions than the Jewish groom, not only because she's the bride and reads the bridal books, but just like Bernie said, because it takes an effort to be a Jewish-Catholic couple. The bride feels, this is what my husband is, I want to learn what his background is, I want to know what his traditions are. And vice versa, the Jewish side ought to take the same steps forward and learn about the richness of the Catholic tradition as well. And again, it's a process--it's not the state of the condition.

MS. SMITH: Couples will say how do you say you are Catholic and Jewish if you're baptized, and how can my child be both?

FATHER BERNIE PIETRZAK: Baptism begins a journey in faith. It's not the defining moment. The Catholic parent, through Baptism, is making a promise to share the experience of their relationship with Jesus Christ with their child. Now whether that child ultimately accepts that and confirms that in their young adult years remains to be seen. But as we talk about it, in the Jewish-Catholic moment, it's not exclusive, it's inclusive. I always tell a couple, when a Catholic person signs that promise before they're married to have their child baptized and raised as a Catholic, I would say that Rabbis I know will say if the Jews were big on paperwork, they'd have the same document! You can be raised in both. Ultimately, they may choose, but who knows what is believed.

RABBI MISHA TILLMAN: One can be educated in both traditions and exposed to both traditions and raised --

FATHER BERNIE PIETRZAK: And celebrate both traditions and be immersed in both traditions.

RABBI MISHA TILLMAN: That's right, that's right.

FATHER BERNIE PIETRZAK: And it's a part of who you are.

RABBI MISHA TILLMAN: Then when one becomes an adult, one, of course, takes responsibility for one's own actions and spiritual path -- you know, these are their own connections and other ways of connecting to the Deity ---it could be Buddhism after all!

FATHER BERNIE PIETRZAK: But also to recognize that, how do we not know that this is God's initiative in the moment of even this grass-roots movement?

MS. SMITH: Let's take an example. A couple has celebrated this ceremony, but then moves to a small town and their new Rabbi doesn't understand what they're doing. Can you help explain this to other clergy people?

RABBI MISHA TILLMAN: Well, in the case of Judaism, every Rabbi follows his or her own convictions. It is not uncommon to run into a Rabbi who not only doesn't understand, he just simply will not want to accept it. He will understand what they're doing, but he will not be willing to accept. In other words, it's perfectly conceivable to run into a Rabbi who will say, "Well, I'm very concerned with the survival of the Jewish people... what you're doing, you're assimilating the Jewish people and contributing to the self-destruction of the Jewish people." I don't agree necessarily with his exposition, but this is what you are likely to hear. Most Rabbis who would officiate at an interfaith wedding would not commit themselves to perform a baby naming baptism ceremony. This is still a very, very, pioneering effort that we're engaged in here. While it depends on the individual Rabbi, overall the Jewish establishment is extremely opposed to anything even remotely resembling this kind of activity and makes the best effort to marginalize this phenomenon which, of course, like all similar campaigns will end up nowhere. When something emerges by itself, when there is a true spiritual need there, you can't eliminate it by ignoring it.

FATHER BERNIE PIETRZAK: You can't put ketchup back in a bottle either.

RABBI MISHA TILLMAN: That's right, exactly, that's well put. It is very unfortunate, but this is what the Jewish establishment is right now. We'll just have to face the reality that those couples who are pursuing this will also encounter misunderstandings, misperception, you know, misconceived notions, and sometimes rejection on behalf of the Jewish establishment. Some Rabbis will accept you, but you have to come into a "one religion" household where, in other words, you should not be practicing Catholicism, that sort of thing. One has just to be prepared to face this. It does take an effort and yes, at times it does take courage.

MS. SMITH: And you advise them to persevere?

RABBI MISHA TILLMAN: Yes I do, only through affirming who you are and getting comfortable with what you do and with your own identity. Don't let them make you feel guilty. They are the ones who are perplexed, not you.

FATHER BERNIE PIETRZAK: I think the other thing you can say too, that within the Catholic tradition, every Catholic priest is able, and is encouraged to share in the celebration of marriage. You're going to find clergy who either by their experience or their fear or their concern, will step back from being involved. If you're creative, you're going to find the people that will support you. More and more I find that as I hear and read things from couples, there are many Rabbis across the country who are open to this. Sometimes you have to find a Rabbi from a big town to come in -- and to enlarge the small town's perspective.

RABBI MISHA TILLMAN: That's true when it comes to weddings, yes. Baby namings, baptisms, the number is, I'm afraid, extremely limited.

FATHER BERNIE PIETRZAK: I would agree with you there, but I think it's limited because of --

RABBI MISHA TILLMAN: Novelty.

FATHER BERNIE PIETRZAK: Novelty or people hadn't considered it as a possibility.

MS. SMITH: Rabbi, what about the parent who feels profoundly Jewish and is worried about their ancestry, their family members perhaps that were killed in the Holocaust? This can be a very challenging time for an interfaith family. Could you speak to that?

RABBI MISHA TILLMAN: Yes, this is very sad, this sense of betraying the ancestors or being unfaithful to them. One thing about Judaism, is that Judaism is known as a very iconoclastic tradition. One of the very important characteristic teachings of Judaism is that it continues to reinvent and redefine itself. It seems we are on the verge of a new era --- on the verge of the Jewish community that is being forced, by itself, to re-evaluate itself and to redefine itself. We know that Jewish people marry non-Jews, which in fact is a very common phenomena now, way in excess of 50 percent. We owe it to ourselves to say that the way Judaism will be 20 years from now is not going to be Judaism as it was in 1920, 1930. This will be Judaism in a different time and different place.

Now, this concept of betrayal and rejection, those are, in my opinion, false concepts. That's not how one should look at it. The only way that you can preserve any spiritual life is to look at it in positive terms. Once you have negative terms, once you have a terminology such as betrayal, rejection, throwing out, negating, you are more likely to fail. Negation does not create. Negation only crosses things out. Negation only annihilates things. If really you wish to create a meaningful spiritual life for your family, then you ought to look at your life from a manner of learning, exploration, searching, being on a spiritual quest, and yes, outstretching your hand to someone who comes from a different tradition. Say to yourself, let us explore what is it that unites us, what are the values that are common to the Jews and Christians. And when we find those common values--because they do exist--then we will learn that we can live as a Jew, as a Christian, together without losing what's dear to us. That is the whole idea, not only to retain what's dear to us, but also to develop and to enrich ourselves --- that's the whole concept. In that regard, it's not a matter of betraying ancestors. It's the matter of preserving, affirming what we have, our heritage, honoring the memory of those who perished in the Holocaust, through enriching their traditions, our traditions, through understanding the traditions of the others.

You know, speaking of the Holocaust, obviously the Jewish people suffered tremendous losses then, but let's not forget that there were many Catholics who were killed during World War II. It is quite a well-established fact that every third citizen of Poland was killed, Jews and Catholics. Let us also remember the many positive experiences that happened during that war and that truly religious Catholics helped many Jews escape the persecution of the Nazis. Is that a betrayal of our ancestry? I think not. I think you emphasize those things as you educate yourselves, as a part of the dialogue.

FATHER BERNIE PIETRZAK: It also says how can I be true to my religious tradition? Well, God is the center of your religious tradition. The Shema tells us that God is One. We share a common God, the one God is the God that Christians worship and believe through Christ, but it's the same God that Abraham and Sarah and Moses saw as the path for the Jewish people. It's the same God, so what is God's dream, rather than simply my ancestors? I'd suggest this: if your ancestors, be they Christians or Jews, if they're with God, then they will share in God's enlightenment and view this with great joy and blessing.

RABBI MISHA TILLMAN: Once again, I'll return to what I said earlier. The God of philosophers is the same. If you look at any theological treatise that concerns itself, preoccupies itself with the most important issues about what God is, the concept of

God, you'll find virtually identical themes, with identical terminology. They all speak of the same God, that God is one; they discuss the unity of God, they discuss proofs of existence of God, definition of prophecy, the deepest, most profound intellectual thoughts, accessible to a chosen few, really. But ultimately, it is the same God: there is **one** God. What respective religious traditions provide us with, Jewish and Catholic alike, and others perhaps, are this system of symbols and system of objects, which make for us emotional connections. I've already said those emotional connections are critically important for a human being, for any human being, because no matter how much you value intellect, when we cannot accept something on an emotional level, no argument will convince us otherwise. That is why that emotional connection is critically important to retain. The idea is to retain or for the systems to enable both parties in marriage to retain and enrich those emotional connections. The word here is to affirm and to develop, not to betray or reject. Only by retaining it do you get it. How can you talk about betrayal when we are talking about revival and reformation?

FATHER BERNIE PIETRZAK: The only comment that I would make in this conversation is this: ritual moments, like sacraments, I believe, come out of a community. They're not individual moments. What I would simply say to young parents regarding baby naming christenings is that, in my mind, it doesn't make a lot of sense to engage in these celebrations if in your mind, there isn't a desire to become part of the synagogue and the Catholic faith community that we call a parish. And if you're seeing that you're not going to be part of these communities, then these individual moments really make no sense. These moments mean everything when they're connected -- when they're connecting you to a people who support, challenge, encourage you in the ways of faith and God when things get challenging or difficult. If you're not part of that people, be it the synagogue or the church, in a way that's going to be helpful, then these are simply superstitious, kinds of --

RABBI MISHA TILLMAN: Going through with the motions.

FATHER BERNIE PIETRZAK: Going through motions that represent, on a very superficial level, parts of our tradition. Because the deeper part of both of our traditions is that we belong to a people, that's where God is found.

MS. SMITH: Thank you both very much.

Where Do We Go From Here?

Faith is a verb. Faith is a way of behaving, which involves knowing, being and willing. The content of faith is best described in terms of our worldview and value system, but faith itself is something we do. Faith is an action. It results from our actions with each other, it changes and expands through our actions with each other, and it expresses itself daily in our actions with each other. No one can determine another's faith and no one can give another faith, but we can be faithful and share our life and faith with one another. Others, regardless of age, can do the same with us, and through this sharing we each sustain, transmit and expand our faith.[1]

Rev. John C. Westerhoff, III

So where do we go from here? The ceremony is concluded, the remnants of the celebratory meal finished, thank you notes have been sent and the business of being a family attentive to its spiritual needs begins in earnest. Before we take a look at the specifics, let's pause for a moment and remember some ideas to keep in mind as we proceed.

Please remember we are talking about faith. We are not so much concerned about membership in a particular club, or checking off certain milestones; nor are we keeping score of how many Catholic or Jewish prayers we have memorized. Rather, we want to teach our children how to discern God's presence in the ordinary aspects of life: we want them to make holy the commonplace. Dr. Rachel Naomi Remen, writing in *Kitchen Table Wisdom* (Riverhead Books, 1996), states, "People can most easily recognize God's presence when it manifests itself in dramatic ways: the person who heals for unknown reasons when all hope is gone, the angelic visitation, the life-altering coincidence. We seem to be able to hear God best when he shouts. Yet the experience of God may be as common as a trip to the grocery store...perhaps the wisdom lies not in the constant struggle to bring the Holy into daily life, but in the recognition that there may be no daily life, that life is committed and whole, and despite appearances, we are always on sacred ground."[2] The trick is to identify and ritualize those daily aspects of life, which put us in touch with that reality. But more on that in a moment.

John Westerhoff, the above-noted theologian, likens the cycles of faith to rings of a tree.[3] The metaphor is a good one: a tree with only one ring is as much of a tree as those with twenty rings, the latter being a more "expanded" tree, not a better tree; also a tree grows slowly over time, where we see only the resulting expansion. We realize that the tree can't skip rings; it needs to grow in an orderly process, each ring an intrinsic part of the foundation of the one to follow. And most importantly, for a tree to grow it needs the proper setting: should that be lacking, the tree stops growing until the right environment occurs. So it is with faith: when you are a child, your faith is whole and complete as it is, no better or greater than it might be for a more senior individual; for faith to flourish it needs care and tending to – it needs the right environment for activities, educational opportunities and *relationships* for it to develop. At the same time, we don't see faith grow directly, but rather note it to have a gradual expansion over time, building upon an earlier expression, incorporating what came before.

The goal of our understanding and of these activities is to underscore the essence of both Judaism and Catholicism: by making sacred the ways in which we live in this world and the people in it. For our purposes here, we are attending to the needs of the young child: the period of time from birth to age five. This is a time when, according to author and researcher Sophia Cavaletti, "...children have shown me that they are capable of deep religious experience, which I believe means a deep relationship with God...they sense God's presence...they understand and enjoy God's closeness."[4] It is this awareness we want to address and manipulate!   (Theologian Bailey Gillespie offers that most parents become interested in their child's religious development somewhere between the ages of 5-9, which "is 5-9 years too late!"[5]). Both Rev. Gillespie and Dr. Westerhoff remind us at these tender ages, our children will be "borrowing" our faith – that is, all that we do with them and for them, in an environment of love, joy and nourishment, will set the stage for all that follows. Between the ages of infant to kindergartner, the family will **model** for the child the experiences of God: the development of faith at this time has more to do with the attitudes associated with an activity or celebration and the parents' love **for one another** than conceptual understanding or the mastery of a task.

"Searching too hard for God can get in the way of finding him. Sometimes you just have to stop looking and let yourself be taken by surprise. Sometimes God can be as plain as the nose on your face...in several of the books I've read recently, the authors make it clear that this business of finding faith is not an intellectual exercise: you cannot think your way to faith."[6]

So says our narrator in author Diane Schoemperlen's new novel <u>Our Lady of the Lost and Found</u> (Penguin Books, 2001). And that point is what we are now about. With my sincerest apologies to Father Westerhoff (who offers eight definite "areas of formation"), I propose that there are four areas of religious routine which we should experience as interfaith families to foster the development of our faith lives, remembering what we do has the power to shape us. Those four areas of focus are: Worship, Prayer, Ritual with attention to a sacred calendar and Tzedakah (or what we will discuss as charity). Liken the practice of religious routine with an exercise program or the mastery of a foreign language: competency comes only from repetition and dedication. So it is the same with faith formation.

WORSHIP

Let's begin our discussion with some thoughts regarding worship. Before my husband and I had children, sharing our individual liturgies with each other was a simple matter: sometimes he joined me at Mass, most often he didn't. At that time, I had no sense of the meaning, or substance of *Shabbat*. What was important was that we respected each other's choice, and each other's independence. With the arrival of our children, our sense of autonomy was gone, replaced with a sense of

newly forged *community*. What was critical to us both was that we not invent some new religion within our family, but rather find a way of expressing what we had both experienced as children, the faith of our fathers. Using the analogy made earlier of "religions as rafts", picture not a newly redesigned raft, but rather our two distinctive vessels tied tightly together as we made our way to shore!

Having been raised as a devout

churchgoer, the way we began was to do what we knew, or rather to do what I had done as a child: we would attend "services." It was clear the little neighborhood church I would sneak off to by myself would not serve the needs of our family. After attending one Easter Vigil service there, my husband was unwavering in his belief that the bonfire was meant for him! It was at this time we discovered the graceful community of Old St. Pats, which in hindsight embraced our family in its totality from the first moment. And so we began our "experiment": the five of us would go to Mass on a trial basis. I don't know that we had any clear expectations beyond that, but eleven years later it is easy to discern how the experiment became a way of life. Our church experience was one of gracious hospitality in the mode of "all being welcome here", with rousing, hand-clapping, and often concert-level music performance by an outstanding choir and stimulating, enriching sermons by energetic, thoughtful clergy (the fact that the building itself had been established by early Irish settlers only added to its allure!). But what encouraged us to return again and again was the sense of welcome and reception by those around us in the pews, and by the clergy themselves. From the moment we arrived, people were anxious to introduce themselves and made each of us feel as if we belonged there – as if the gifts we brought were just as important as their own. Educators say kids learn not always by what they are taught, but by what is *caught*, and I am often reminded of that at church. Did the children understand what was going on during the consecration of the host? Did they sit still during the sermon, or did their minds not wander? My guess is not all that was *supposed* to happen happened. I will not forget the delight my children displayed when they were called *by name* by the clergy – offered a 'high five' or 'how ya doing in school?' It offered them relationship to a community, a community that held meaning for their parents. And of course that is why they were there. I remember how much I disliked going to church as a child – the mass was distant, in a foreign language and just plain boring. While some of the particulars might be different, there was still reluctance on our children's part to leave their activities, friends, or in some cases, their beds to go to church. And while the case was sometimes made by a bright 5-year-old that "you didn't need to go to a special place to pray to God", the lesson taught had more to do with boundaries, something they were *very* familiar with – time to eat, time to play, time for bed, time for worship.

When young children are invited to celebrate and participate with others present, what transpires is something beyond imagining, something almost mystical. It is true that by the time we figured out what we needed to be doing as a family, our children were five, four and almost one. I remember vividly the image of our baby, propped in a backpack, nibbling on pretzel rods over my shoulder for the first few months we were in attendance. Despite their ages, I must believe there was a purpose in their presence there. I can only hope that what our children caught at those ages was something akin to inclusion and delight: we were having a meaningful time experiencing excellent worship *together*. If our goals were to have our family fluent in certain practices, well, using the metaphor of language, this could only happen by 'speaking the language' – by doing worship!

I would be lying if I said my husband and I didn't have a conversation about "balancing" our religious traditions. If we went to church, didn't that mean we should also go to temple? Even though this ritual had NOT been his practice as a child, he now felt driven to attend Friday night services. We spent the next year or so visiting different shuls, meeting with the rabbis until we found a temple we felt comfortable in, a temple which, coincidentally, was home to many interfaith families. When we began our 'organized' commitment to religious practice, my husband and I would attend Friday night services together, without the children. Being the Catholic partner, I didn't know much about the home celebration of Shabbat (whose preparation falls to the mom) and using the Catholic paradigm set out to shul. Routinely, we would make a date to attend services together; it was only the rare occasion or holiday that we gathered up our children to celebrate the Sabbath with us at services.

One such occasion happened years ago during the celebration of the Jewish festival of *Simchat Torah*. This was to be a special event in the life of our temple, for this year, we were receiving a new Torah, one which had been rescued from Czechoslovakia during World War II. Appropriately, this holiday commemorates reading the final verses from the book of Deuteronomy (which tells of the death of Moses) and begins the scripture cycle again at the beginning of Genesis. As our new Torah was in dire straights when we first received it, a scribe had been commissioned to restore it, with the final period at the end of the last sentence to be added at the festival. So, on a beautiful fall evening, not expecting too much out of the ordinary, our family headed out to temple.

What happened next was anything but ordinary. The Rabbi had invited the sole Jewish survivor from the small town of Poidivin, where the Torah had belonged. As the services unfolded, our family was privileged to participate in an experience of great joy. After the reading was complete and the final punctuation mark added, the Torah was unfurled around the perimeter of the room, with all in attendance given a portion to hold as they too spread out to the far reaches of the sanctuary. As the scroll was rewound, the rabbi visited each eager participant and shared with the congregation what portion they were holding! Once the rewinding of the Torah was complete, our honored guest from a foreign land led a joyful, riotous procession of dancing and clapping around the room, to the accompaniment of our temple musicians. To this day, our children will beam when they recall this evening, one that began innocuously, but was in reality filled with the many faces of God.

This celebration was the beginning of our family's commitment to honoring the Sabbath in a meaningful way: it was not long after these festivities that I learned the holiest of holidays is in fact the Sabbath – not Passover, or Yom Kippur, but what Jews all over the world celebrate each Friday night! It was clear after our attendance at Simchat Torah that we *wanted* to participate as a family on a regular basis: it took something as stimulating, challenging and full of surprise to move us to participate more fully. And while I can't say that we attend services *every* week, when we are not at temple, we have crafted our own services at home (which we'll cover later in our section on ritual).

Religious services are the regular articulation of that which we hold up as our ideals and values. It is through the medium of religious services that, collectively, we express what makes us a congregation: public worship is intended to motivate us to act together to fulfill our purposes.

I recently spoke with Rabbi Michael Sternfield, Senior Rabbi of Chicago Sinai Congregation, about the value of worship attendance. While he speaks to the experience at temple, his words cut across individual religious traditions. He said "religious services are the regular articulation of that which we hold up as our ideals and values. It is through the medium of religious services that, collectively, we express what makes us a congregation: public worship is intended to motivate us to act together to fulfill our purposes. Public worship is not an end in itself; it is a means to an end. We are not just holding services because that is what we always do – we conduct public worship because this is what expresses best who we are and what we stand for."[7] His colleague Rabbi Howard Berman, Rabbi Emeritus at Sinai, agrees, echoing, "(Worship) is the setting in which, through the inspiration of prayer and music, we can develop and deepen our belief. It is the means through the instruction and challenge from the pulpit that we nurture the intellectual foundation of our commitment."[8] Tom McGrath, contributing editor of *U.S. Catholic,* recently spoke to the issue of worship, saying, "Our culture is full of empty promises, and (Sunday) worship is transforming, for it is the most powerful event to give us eyes to see the emptiness."[9] Father John Cusick, Director of the Young Adult Ministry Office of the Archdiocese of Chicago and chaplain to interfaith families, concurs and feels there are multi-faceted reasons for participating in weekly worship, reasons as fundamental to life as breathing. "You must remember that our ancestors believed that you couldn't keep a significant promise more than a week, so once a week they assembled to renew the promise to be God's great, faithful people. In today's culture, I believe there is a similar 'spin': regular worship is needed to remind us of who we are and what we are called to do with our lives. On a personal level, I understand there is a divine presence as close as the food I eat that is there for me in good times and in bad. No matter where I am in my own life, I am told that I am loved, that I am somebody special, a beloved child of God. And in a world that keeps demanding you be just like everyone else, I (am reminded that I) am called to greatness. You cannot be great in this world by yourself; it just doesn't work. I need to know that there are other people like me with whom I can be in community, with whom I can worship and with whom I can share the greatness, the call to greatness in God. In addition, you can't say that you are a follower or a disciple if you never sit down and eat with the master!"[10] Rabbi Harold Kushner speaks to the issue of community in his book *To Life!* (Warner Books, 1994), saying, "Congregating is at least as important as the prayers we offer. Praying with a congregation offers us the message that we are not alone in our hopes, our fears, our aspirations. It invites us to transcend our individual isolation and lose ourselves in a group, to experience the sense of being a part of something greater than ourselves."[11]

There is one other thought that I might offer regarding an unforeseen benefit of routine attendance at worship services. After years of attendance, you come to recognize the ebb and flow of the service: the prayers, blessings, readings and responses become second nature. But what also comes with familiarity is similarity. The responses we say at mass, "pray that our sacrifice may be acceptable to God", will be repeated at the Shabbat service on Friday evening, when we say "Our God, grant that our worship on this Sabbath be acceptable to you." When we chant *Kadosh, kadosh, kadosh Adonai tz'va-ot, m'lo kol ha-ah-retz k'vo-do* (Holy, holy, holy is the God of all creation. The whole universe is full of God's glory) during the celebration of a Jewish festival, we are delighted to hear *Holy Holy Holy Lord God power and might, heaven and earth are filled with your glory* at mass. The concurrence of such statements, with the underpinnings of awe and surprise, can only challenge and move our faith lives further along in our family's understanding of our one God.

For it is in the community's liturgy, story and actions merge; in worship we remember and we act in symbolic ways that bring our sacred tradition and our lives together, providing us with both meaning and motivation for daily existence. That is why, if our children are to have faith, they must worship with us.

We will give the last word to the work of John Westerhoff, whose words opened this chapter. Again, in his seminal book, *Will Our Children Have Faith?* he states, "...for it is in the community's liturgy, story and actions merge; in worship we remember and we act in symbolic ways which bring our sacred tradition and our lives together, providing us with both meaning and motivation for daily existence. That is why, if our children are to have faith, they must worship with us."[12]

PRAYER

From my earliest memories, I can't remember a time when I didn't pray. I recall the childish prayer at bedtime, seeking safety from the 'bogey-man' in "Now I lay me down to sleep, I pray the Lord my soul to keep" to the more *adult* prayer of bribing God with a pledge of a rosary if only I made it into my high school choir! Of course, this was the 50's and 60's, and I had been fed a healthy dose of the Baltimore Catechism to accompany all my pleadings.

While that formational manual may not be in usage much among our interfaith families during this new millennium, the basic tenets regarding prayer are still held dear within the Catechism of the Catholic Church. As an adult now, when I re-read the text, I am reminded of those *forms* of prayer I was taught as a child. For a brief review, there are five: the first kinds of prayer are those of **adoration,** or those prayers of love and devotion, acknowledging God's supremacy and sovereignty such as we might find in the psalms (e.g. *For King of all the earth is God; sing hymns of praise. God reigns* 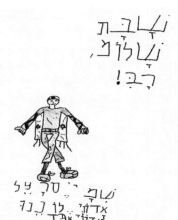 *over the nations, God sits upon his holy throne. The princes of the peoples are gathered together with the people of the God of Abraham. For God's are the guardians of the earth; He is supreme.)*[13]; the second kinds of prayer are those of **petition** and are probably most familiar to us, for they are those that seek *something* ---to recover from an illness, to get a good grade on an important test, to land a certain job, for a healthy baby, (to get into choir!) and so forth. And while these prayers are always about our needs, I remember needing to be reminded to add "according to your will, O Lord." The third kinds of prayers are those of gratitude or **thanksgiving.** Kay Bracco, a religious educator in Chicago and mother of ten, reports a story told to her by *her* grandmother when she was a child. "Every day, God sends two angels down to earth, each with a basket. One angel, George, has a huge basket for *petitions*; the other, Gertrude, has a smaller one for *thanksgivings*. By 10 in the morning, George's basket is so full he has to go back to heaven to dump out all the petition prayers, then return to Earth for more. Poor Gertrude, when she goes back to heaven at night with her little basket, there are only a couple of thanksgiving prayers in it."[14] We forget to say 'thank you' even when we have received the very thing we are looking for – let alone for banquets of plenty not sought. The fourth forms of prayer are those of **forgiveness,** to offer "I'm sorry" to neighbor and God alike. The more formal and traditional of these prayers are plentiful in both

Christian and Jewish liturgy and have been so ingrained in our memory that they come to mind easily. It might be on the Day of Atonement Yom Kippur, where the day is one of reparation and apology and we say, "We call you Avinu; as a loving parent, forgive our sins and failings, and reach for us as we reach for you"[15], or the Act of Contrition I learned as a child, preparing for the sacrament of penance, reciting, "Oh my God, I am heartily sorry for having offended thee." The fifth and final forms of prayer are those of **praise**. By definition, according to the catechism, these are prayers that "laud God for his own sake and gives him glory, quite beyond what he does, but simply because HE IS."[16]   For those looking through a Catholic lens, we understand the gift of the Eucharist to be the 'sacrifice of praise'; at the same time, for the Jewish people, the Sh'ma is the holist of prayers, saying *Ba-ruch Shem K'vod mal-chu-to l'olam va-ed (Let us praise God who rules in glory forever and ever).*

But we are no longer children, and our prayer life should reflect the same. A new, applicable and pervasive model of prayer needs to be understood. Father John Cusick proposes a new way of thinking of prayer, which he suggests is "practicing the presence of God", and which he admits "takes practice and consistency."[17] Rabbi Harold Kushner offers a like-minded working definition in the statement "it is not talking to God so much as it is using words and music to come into the presence of God in the hope that we will be changed by doing so."[18]

He believes that in Judaism "a prayer is answered not when we get what we were asking for, but when we are granted a sense of God's nearness...for example (sic), the prayer of a sick person is 'answered' not by having his disease disappear, but by gaining the sense of God's nearness, the assurance that his illness is not a punishment from God and that God has not abandoned him."[19]

When I was a child, I remember the emphasis on proper posture and kneeling at prayer times. With my own children I am more aware of the power of a stroke of the hand, the force of a gentle caress, the gift of an embrace as I teach them the experience of God's presence through prayer.

Now we are parents as well as adults; what do we want to teach our children about prayer? How do we go about teaching them, showing them that God is as present as their very breath?

I think there are a few basic rules we can use, the first of which is Keep It Simple. For our pre-kindergarteners, we know it is <u>not</u> about understanding metaphors or symbols, nor the acquisition of religious knowledge. This time of faith formation is best described as being feelings-oriented or relational. In the jargon of the developmental specialists, this is the time the child orders his world regarding trusting behavior for the *rest of his life!* Therefore, this time spent as a family should be conducive to holding and touching one another; this is a time for singing, and clapping and delighting *together.* When I was a child, I remember the emphasis on proper posture and kneeling at prayer times. With my own children I am more aware of the power of the stroke of a hand, the force of a gentle caress, the gift of an embrace as I teach them the experience of God's presence through prayer.

The second rule to consider is the belief that "we become that which we behold", or said differently, children learn what they experience. They won't get it if YOU don't do it! Theologian Bailey Gillespie, who we met in an earlier chapter, states, "We do not learn about God at first through some knowledge of God's revelation. Rather, we teach our children about God by the way we are. Another person's lived faith is the *modus operandi* of religious experience during this initial faith situation."[20] We must become the model for our children, for they will only know to do what we have done for *and* with them.

To this day, my favorite prayer said to my children is the following (with my apologies to the author): "And in God's house, in His bedroom, on His dresser, is a picture of *you.*" What a lovely image with which to drift off to sleep!

The third theory is simply to identify those moments, experiences and situations throughout the day with your child that will keep you mindful of being in a relationship with God (that goes beyond our tone of voice, how we care for one another and how we treat one another.). Be mindful not to give the impression that there are only certain times at which we pray (silence too is prayer!). Scholar Sofia Cavaletti tells of the importance of parents educating their children to *prayer* and not to prayer<u>s</u>. "What the adult can do is to establish the premises that will help prayer to arise. Such premises should be as indirect in character as possible, so as to allow the greatest space for the child's personal response."[21] For example, when our children wake for the day, we need to greet them with joy, blessing them and giving thanks for "the sunny skies God has given us" or "the rain which gently bathes the flowers" on that morn. As we do our errands with them riding beside us in the car, we need to be attentive to our language towards other drivers and grateful for arriving at our destination safely, announcing a quiet "Thank you, Lord." At meals, we need to give thanks around the table, blessing each other and the food to be shared, as well as those who do not share in such a bounty each day. To this day, my teenage children are not ashamed or embarrassed (or so they tell me!) when we go out to eat in a restaurant as we gather each other's hands to say grace. Praying at meals, like wearing a seatbelt when in a car, has become a natural and permanent activity. When our children were quite little, the evening always seemed to hold a mystical, sacred quality. Each evening as they begin to quiet for the night, the routine always included a quiet song, or story whose theme included God's loving kindness. This was the time for cuddling and holding, for forging those intimate bonds representative of divine love, underscoring the belief that life is good. When the children were a bit older and language was more developed, this was the time to share the stories of our day: to do our bidding one more time, to say "I love you", to say "I'm sorry", to say "I'm glad God gave you to me." To this day, my favorite prayer said to my children is the following (with my apologies to the author): "And in God's house, in His bedroom, on His dresser, is a picture of *you*." What a lovely image with which to drift off to sleep.

If our final goal is that our children have a relationship with an Almighty Being, then it is our task to teach them how to practice the presence of God. And while the emphasis is on making sacred the ordinary, as language develops, common prayers can be learned over time, not necessarily through memorization but rather through natural repetition. What is key is that our children's natural inclination to prayer be encouraged. That being said, what follows below is a short list of the most common traditional prayers within Catholicism and Judaism. These prayers are those that are central to the core of both religious traditions that our children will hear and *use* as their faith lives evolve. Years ago, our children learned the prayers said on Shabbat for the blessing over the wine, the Kiddush. When the Kiddush was said at temple during the *Oneg Shabbat*, they were elated that they could say the words along with the rabbi – words that were foreign to many of those gathered around them! Knowledge of these prayers gave them the tools to operate as a part of the immediate assemblage, as well as the ability to relate to an ancient community of people. We should not take this privilege of instruction lightly, or for granted.

APOSTLES' CREED	
	I believe in God, the Father Almighty, creator of heaven and earth. I believe in Jesus Christ, his only Son, our Lord. He was conceived by the power of the Holy Spirit and born of the Virgin Mary. He suffered under Pontius Pilate, was crucified, died and was buried. He descended into hell. On the third day, He arose again. He ascended into heaven and is seated at the right hand of the Father. He will come again to judge the living and the dead. I believe in the Holy Spirit, the holy catholic Church, the communion of saints, the forgiveness of sins, the resurrection of the body, and of life everlasting. Amen.
AVINU MALKAYNU (Prayer said for the ten days of repentance)	Avino Mal-kay-nu, cha-nay-nu va-ah-nay-nu, Ke ayn ba-nu ma-ah-seem. Ah-say ee-ma-nu ts'da-kah va-che-sed v'ho-she-ay-nu. Avinu Malkaynu, be gracious to us and answer us, for there is little merit in us. Treat us generously and with kindness and be our help.
BLESSING OVER THE CANDLES (Sabbath)	Ba-ruch Atah Adonai Elo-hay-nu Melech ha-olam, ah-share kid-shanu b'mitz-vo-tav, V'tzi-va-nu l'had-leek nayr shel Shabbat.

	We praise You, eternal God, Ruler of the Universe, who hallows us through laws and ethical teachings, and commands us to kindle the Sabbath lights.
BLESSING OVER THE CHALLAH	Ba-ruch Atah Adonai Elo-hay-nu Me-lech ha-olam, Ha-mo-tzee le-chem min ha-ah-retz. Let us praise the Eternal God, Ruler of the Universe, Who brings forth bread from the earth.

BLESSING OVER THE CHILDREN (Shabbat)	May God bless you and Guide you. Be strong for the truth, charitable in your words, just and loving in your deeds. A precious heritage has been entrusted to you. Guard it well.
GLORY TO GOD (said at Catholic Mass)	Glory to God in the highest, and peace to his people on earth. Lord God, heavenly King, almighty God and Father, we worship you, we give you thanks, we praise you for your glory. Lord Jesus Christ, only Son of the Father, Lord God, Lamb of God, you take away the sin of the world: have mercy on us. You are seated at the right hand of the Father, receive our prayer. For you alone are the Holy One, you alone are the Lord, you alone are the most high, Jesus Christ, with the Holy Spirit, in the glory of God the Father. Amen.
HAIL MARY	Hail Mary, full of grace, the Lord is with you. Blessed are you among women, and blessed is the fruit of your womb, Jesus. Holy Mary, Mother of God, pray for our sinners, now and at the hour of our death. Amen.

HINEI MA TOV	Hi-nei mah tov u-mah na-im, she-vet achim gam ya-chad How good it is and lovely, for people to dwell together.
KIDDUSH	Ba-ruch Atah Adonai, Elo-hay-nu Melech ha-olam, ah-share kid-sh-nu b'mitz-vo-tav v'ra-tzah va-nu. V'Shabbat kod-sho, b'ah-ha-vah uv-ra-tzon hin-chee-lan-nu, zee-ka-ron l'ma-ah-say v-ray-sheet. Ke hu yom t-chee-lah, l'mik-ra-ay ko-desh, zay-cher lee-tzee-aht mit-ra-yeem. Ke va-nu va-chart-ta v'oh-ta-nu kee-dash-ta, me-kol ha-ah-meem, v'Shabbat kod-sh'cha b'ah-ha-vah uv'ra-tzon hin-chal-ta-nu. Baruch Atah Adonai, m'ka-daysh ha-Shabbat. Blessed is the Eternal God, Ruler of the Universe, who hallows us through the commandments and takes delight in us. In love and favor, God has made holy the Sabbath our heritage, as a reminder of the work of creation. It is first among our sacred days, a remembrance of the Exodus from Egypt. O God, You have called us from among all people, and in love and favor have given us the Sabbath day as a sacred inheritance. We thank You, O God, for the Sabbath and its holiness.

NICENE CREED (said at Catholic Mass)	We believe in one God, the Father, the Almighty, maker of heaven and earth, of all that is seen and unseen. We believe in one Lord, Jesus Christ, the only Son of God, eternally begotten of the Father, God from God, Light from Light, true God from true God, not made, one in Being with the Father through whom all things were made. For our sake and for our salvation he came down from heaven; by the power of the Holy Spirit he was born of the Virgin Mary, and became man. For our sake, He was crucified under Pontius Pilate; he suffered, died and was buried. On the third day he rose again in fulfillment of the Scriptures; he ascended into heaven and is seated at the right hand of the Father. He will come again in glory to judge the living and the dead, and His kingdom will have no end. We believe in the Holy Spirit, the Lord, the giver of life, who proceeds from the Father and the Son. With the Father and the Son He is worshipped and glorified. He has spoken through the Prophets. We believe in one holy catholic and apostolic Church. We acknowledge one baptism for the forgiveness of sins. We look for the resurrection of the dead, and the life of the world to come. Amen.
	"Our Father, who art in heaven, hallowed be Thy name. Thy kingdom

OUR FATHER	come, thy will be done, on earth, as it is in heaven. Give us this day our daily bread; and forgive us our trespasses as we forgive those who trespass against us; and lead us not into temptation, but deliver us from evil. For Thine is the kingdom and the power and the glory, now and forever. Amen.
SHEHECHEYANU	Ba-ruch Atah Adonai Elo-hay-nu Melech ha-o-lam, Sh'he-chee-ya nu v'kee-yma nu v'he-gee-ya-nu laz-man ha-zeh. Let us praise God, Ruler of the universe, for giving us life, for sustaining us, and for enabling us to reach this day.
THE SHEMA	Shema Yisrael Adonai Elohaynu Adonai Echad Ba-ruch Shem K'Vod mal-chu-to l'olam va-ed Hear O Israel, The Eternal is our God, The eternal God is One. Let us praise God who rules in glory forever and ever.
THE SIGN OF THE CROSS	In the name of the Father, and of the Son, and of the Holy Spirit. Amen.

RITUAL

Ritual. When we hear the word, an image immediately springs to mind of some activity, perhaps one we recollect from our childhood. My own memories are those of Christmas. Growing up, I bet we were the only children who never participated in decorating the family tree. In fact, we never saw the tree standing decorated till late Christmas morning! It had been my parent's tradition to keep everything secret – long after the tree had been purchased and relegated to stand in a pot of water out in the backyard. Late Christmas Eve, after all of the kids

had been put to bed, my parents brought in the tree and spent their evening decorating with gusto. We let our imaginations run wild as we stayed in our rooms, listening to the sounds emanating from the living room. Our morning routine was just as disciplined: we awoke on Christmas morning, got ready for church and marched out the door *blindfolded,* past the tree and the promise it held. Upon returning from mass, we changed from our Sunday best, ate breakfast and only THEN were permitted to run into the room to see what Santa had left behind. While it might sound restrictive now, it was in fact a magical time, one of great anticipation and expectation, mystery and joy. And it was our *tradition.*

So what exactly are rituals: what is their ultimate purpose? Author Laura Bernstein, writing in a collection of essays regarding spirituality, speaks to the definition of ritual, saying, "Ritual is the enactment of a tradition's basic symbols (the connecting links to Ultimacy) and myths (the symbols in narrative form) by a community of practitioners…the purpose of ritual is to allow the external structure to bring us closer to the internal workings of Ultimate Reality. Put another way, it is to enable us to be more God-centered in our daily lives. Rituals are reminders of who we are and where we come from. If used to their fullest capacity, they can steer us on our path to deeper encounters with what makes life worth living: realms of mystery that include love, faith, awe, and interconnectedness." [22] Rabbi Lawrence Kushner has a similar understanding of religious ritual in that it offers a new perception of life. "It could be dietary, charitable or liturgical. They all set life in a new perspective. Nothing physically changes: everything remains just as it has been. Sleeping, washing, eating, doing the dishes --- only now these things are done from a new vantage point in a different mode...religious rituals are a funny sequence of things we do to help us remember that we have forgotten why we have been created and gently supply us with the instruments of return."[23]

Most simply, rituals don't make things holy, but rather they are the reminder that we have the power to identify the ordinary as sacred. My children know this as the "R" rule: rituals = reminders! Whether we are reluctant beginners or eager starters, how do we find our way to seeing with new eyes? To begin, here are a few strategies to guide us:

- Know yourself, know what you are about. Be sincere in your commitment to learn and grow, for if you feel you are proceeding because you *should*, chances are you'll fail before too long (due to the energy and interest required.) Begin your journey because you want to, and not for some (or somebody's) external expectation. I remember years ago, before we were members of a synagogue, one Rabbi that my husband and I were consulting encouraged my husband to join the temple, just "to get his feet wet." Using his simile, I said "Rabbi, forget about the pool - I think Steve is still in the locker room deciding whether or not to get changed into his bathing suit!" While the story might seem corny, the point was until *Steve* knew where he was headed and what he wanted, he couldn't respond to some external pressure for a change in his behavior.

- Begin slowly. When confronted with the newness of change, one sometimes has the tendency to be overwhelmed. Be mindful of God's presence in the ordinary, awkward, beautiful, painful, boring moments of everyday. Realize that your family doesn't have to join the seminary or a convent to encounter a valuable experience--which leads us to our next suggestion, which is:

- Keep it simple. Remember, with young children the key is feelings and attitudes, rather than about knowing things.

Decide on those things that are shared experiences, whether it's eating or bedtime (which we'll discuss specifically below) and build around them. Often it's easier to create family rituals around those activities that are in themselves routine, rather than a holiday that comes once a year. For example, while it is fine and good to establish a particular ritual around Hanukkah or Advent, by the time the holiday returns the following year, you will only have to "re-create" it. On the positive side, however, use these annual events as a building block. Perhaps it is awkward to light the holiday candles at first, but over time, you become extremely comfortable with your evolving custom and are able to add new traditions piece by piece, sustained by new competence.

- Don't compare yourselves to others. In a world such as ours, the likelihood is that you will come to know one or many interfaith families like yourselves. The surest way to feel badly about the path your family has taken, or how you choose to live out that routine is to compare yourself to others. What is right for one family is not going to be right for yours. While it is fine to share information, suggestions and practices, be sure not to add a "value" to them and think that one way is "better" than the next. Do something that *your* family will enjoy.

- The corollary to the above approach is there isn't one right way to do things. Be creative as a family in how you choose to celebrate your relationship with God. As your children grow, tap into their imaginations, their innocence, their understanding of God in their lives. All it takes is desire and interest (and stamina, so be careful not to burnout!).

- Turn off the television set!

- Finally, let go. It is not our place to decide where our child's imagination will go; no one can lead the mysterious invention of a child.

Armed with those few suggestions, let's look at those arenas in our lives where we might introduce ritual into our young families.

The first place that is conducive to integrating tradition is **bedtime.** While the schedule of a young child's day often affords many opportunities for bedtime rites (mornings, naptimes, etc.), it is nighttime that can provide the most powerful glimpse into the extraordinary and sacred. From the time my children were infants, singing to them became the cornerstone of our bedtime routine (in fact, there were times when I felt moved to tears from the strength of the emotion, holding them gently against my cheek, smelling their sweet heads, as they drifted off to sleep.). As they grew older and became more fluent with language, storytelling and reading were important pieces of our routine. If I were not too mentally 'challenged' by the end of the day, I would create my own stories, often making my child the hero or heroine of that particular tale. Fortunately, there are many wonderful books for children, including *Does God have a Big Toe?* by Rabbi Marc Gellman; *Stories of Jesus* by William Griffin; and several of the books written by Sandy Eisenberg Sasso, such as *God's Paintbrush* and *In God's Name*;  which speak to the child of God's loving kindness and inclusion. I must admit I, too, did not teach my children formal prayers: instead, they were encouraged to speak to God in their words, focusing on giving thanks, praise and requests. By the time they were preschoolers, we often spoke about the highlights of our day and the times when we could have made better choices or done a better job. Needless to say, there were endless hugs and kisses before the evening could be concluded. (In fact, we created a blessing ritual where we touched each other on the forehead, offering to each other the gift of God's peace and protection.) Time and time again, the message conveyed through all these activities was our (and intrinsically God's) <u>unconditional</u> love of them.

Another occasion to make sacred the ordinary is **mealtime.** Even before we had children, my husband and I always prayed at mealtimes.

When they were very small, we continued our habit, as we felt it was important for them to experience us praying; to see us hold hands and turn our attentions elsewhere. As they grew, they joined us in our prayers, first in a more formal rote thanksgiving, soon followed by a 'free-form' prayer, where each person was allowed the opportunity to speak from their heart, mindful of the blessings of our day. Regardless of what words were spoken, the respect, quiet attention, and mindfulness of God's abundance were ever-present. Be forewarned, though, of the stares you may receive in McDonald's or Burger King should you choose to carry this ritual outside of your home. We wanted to be consistent with our children, so regardless of where we ate, we took our blessings with us. In addition, I must admit we are blessed (and lucky) in that, to this day, we have been able to eat dinner every night together as a family. It is the usual occurrence that we are gathered around the table sharing a meal and each other's lives. (Modern social scientists will tell us that the sign of the healthiest families are those that eat dinner together – **NOT** those that attend church, or coach soccer, or act as room parents!)

While we touched on the importance of ritual worship before, it cannot be overstated. Theologian John Westerhoff states "to cease worshipping is to lose faith...to transmit faith to the next generation is to include them as participants in all the community's rituals."[24] Whether we choose to celebrate the Sabbath as Shabbat (from Friday night at sundown till Saturday night at sundown), Sunday the 'Lord's Day', or both, taking time out of the week and **making the Sabbath sacred** is a simple gift you can give to your family. Our family came to the discussion of the Sabbath when our children were beyond the pre-school years. When they were very little, I attended mass by myself, and Friday nights came and went. Since that time, however, we have discovered the intrinsic beauty and celebration in setting aside Friday night apart from all other nights. Whether you decide to have a theme Shabbat (pizza Shabbat, pajama Shabbat, etc), this is a holy day that families can make their own. Turn off the phone and the television. Perhaps you set the table with a nicer place setting, or use a special pair of candlesticks, or the children get "crystal" instead of plastic (well, okay--plastic that looks like crystal!): all these things will turn a meal into a sacrament. Be sure to say the prayers welcoming in the Sabbath as you light the candles, and to bless each other before you bless the wine and the challah (both these readings are found in the prayer index above). We have tried to honor the rest of the evening with family time: perhaps with a few more stories read in mom and dad's bed, maybe it was singing while they were in the bathtub, or maybe it was a family game, suitable for all ages. (Now that our children are older, we still reserve Shabbat as "our" time, and restrict activities that take us away from one another.) All of these activities sustain and strengthen our relationship with one another, as well as with our God.

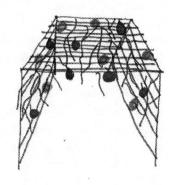

Once we decided we would celebrate the Sabbath, we determined we would go to mass too, together. What was of utmost importance was to find a church we could feel comfortable and welcome in *together*. I am not reluctant to admit we did a bit of church 'shopping', for we understood how important it was going to be for us to worship together, in a community that would be welcoming to both an interfaith couple and one with young children. In the worship section above, I spoke at some length of the loving community we encountered at Old St. Patrick's Church in Chicago. We have maintained our schedule of weekly worship, sometimes followed by lunch.

Someone asked me once how we deal with the kids' activities (whether sports or other) conflicting with church, and for us, the answer was easy. It was and is simply a matter of priorities: we felt we needed as many tools as possible in our arsenal to combat a very shallow culture, one that strives to devalue the lives of our children. Time for all the glorious symbols of ritual worship and being together help us combat what is becoming society's norm.

Both Jewish tradition and Catholic belief is laden with ritual. Whether it's through rites of passage (circumcision or baptism for example) or following the sacred story through the holidays and festivals scattered throughout the calendar, there are many opportunities for young families to create their own observances. One of our family's favorite rituals has been to combine the excitement of advent with the blessings of a mitzvot. Every morning during advent, each member of our family would choose a slip of paper from a box sitting on the kitchen table, on which was written a different 'task': feed the dog without being asked, do your sister's chores, say something nice to someone who is excluded from play, compliment your teacher, and so forth. Then each night, the strips of paper were folded into a loop, from which a chain was created. By the time it is Christmas, the chain is lengthy, and is a tangible manifestation of the hundreds of acts of kindness we all performed, committed over the previous month in the spirit of love.

There are many holidays within our two traditions that are pleasing and meaningful to young children: from the glow of the Hanukkah lights while chanting the sacred text, to the glee established when opening the doors on the advent calendar; to the merrymaking, costumes and food during the festival of Purim (where the Jews of Persia were saved from extinction by the courage of Queen Esther near the time of 500 BCE) to the awe and anticipation of Christmas morning, spying the now-occupied manger in the crèche; from the special foods and reading of the Passover Seder to the mindful embrace of Lenten offerings. What is most important is the realization that our family time is precious and we need to be intentional of the rituals we create. As it is often the secular calendar (and the celebration of Halloween, Valentine's Day, Mother's Day, etc.) or the civil calendar (Memorial Day, Labor Day, the 4th of July [Independence Day], etc.) that make demands of us, we need to make a conscientious commitment to the rituals of our sacred calendars which tell our story, if our children are to have faith.

The message simply is this: be confident, and begin. Whether it is a simple kiss as your child returns from preschool or the building of a sukkah in your backyard, realize the power of the ritual life you can create in your own family.

TZEDAKAH

"A rose by any other name…" While the word may be in Hebrew, the meaning is the same in any language, or within any religious tradition. Commonly the word tzedakah is used to mean *charity* (though is translated as *righteousness*) and is made evident by our actions. Those of us who are living in an interfaith family often strive to find the common ground, the similarities between our two religious traditions. The concept of tzedakah is one such tenet.

Looking through the Catholic lens, an epistle of James leaves no room for ambiguity:

But what good is it, my brothers, if someone says he has faith, but does not have works? If a brother or sister has nothing to wear and has no food for the day, and one of you says to them "Go in peace, keep warm, and eat well", but you do not give them the necessities of the body, what good is it? So also faith of itself, if it does not have works, is dead.[25]

Written at about the same time 2000 years ago, one of the Rabbis of the Mishnah taught, *"Ayn Ha-midrash ha-iykar, elah ha-ma-ah-say--It is not the talking which is essential, rather it is the doing."*[26] I would suggest this is the very same concept!

I have come to learn that the Jewish community's sense of itself is to be a partner with God in completing the work of creation; that through *tikkun olam* (literally "fixing the world"), one is challenged to bring peace and wholeness to our broken world. Rabbi Steven Carr Reuben explains it this way: "*Tikkun Olam* decrees that our primary task as human beings is to do whatever we can in our lifetime to bring shalom into this world. We are to repair the fragments of the world we live in – mend the shattered lives around us; bring comfort to the sick at heart; bring healing to the sick of body; bring shelter to the homeless; bring food to the starving; bring clothes to the ragged; bring hope to those in despair."[27] More locally, Rabbi Howard Berman of Chicago Sinai Congregation sees the very essence of Judaism as the centrality of ethical responsibility. "The genius and the glory of Judaism is that from the beginning, it so dramatically broadened the definition of religious commitment --- reclaiming and renewing the ancient Jewish perspective that beyond the foundation of our personal inner faith, and our shared worship and study, the *ultimate* expression of religion is the way in which it motivates and empowers people to join in society's struggle for social justice – for peace – for reconciliation...this is the sacred mandate of our faith."[28]

From my earliest memories as an Irish-Catholic child, the working definition of the gospel of Jesus was to "Love one another as I have loved you." This was easily translated into doing age-appropriate activities: from donating my pennies to the UNICEF box for Trick-or-Treat at Halloween, to donating babysitting money to the Jerry Lewis Muscular Dystrophy telethon, to being of service in a global way by joining the Peace Corps and living and teaching in impoverished Africa.

These activities underscored the lessons I learned in the Baltimore Catechism, formally called the seven corporal works of mercy (to feed the hungry, give drink to the thirsty, clothe the naked, harbor the homeless, visit the sick, to ransom the captive and to bury the dead.)

In **both** religious traditions we are commanded to serve one another. For an interfaith family, celebrating *tzedakah* is an easy, tangible gift we can give to our children, that they might see and experience the power and responsibility we each have to shape our world. Some opportunities that young families have are to:

- Decorate a box that can be used for holding change; each day, drop loose change into the box which will be targeted for donation (if they are old enough for an allowance, decide what portion should be set aside for contribution);

- Decide where the donations will go, and if possible, deliver them in person so the children can see how their money is being used by others;

- Receive presents on their birthdays, but donate their 'gently-used' toys and clothes on their ½ birthdays (although I have fallen into the habit of making or buying ½ a cake on this anniversary, we also pack up the toys and clothes they have outgrown. While it is sometimes hard to let go of some of their 'possessions', the lesson taught is a powerful one);

- Check with local nursing homes to see if they have a policy on visiting with young children; if appropriate, create an afternoon of reading (check ahead with Catholic Charities, or the Council for Jewish Elderly on specific sites);

- Tap into the resources of your local temple and church for family-friendly activities to serve those less fortunate.

The key to all of these activities is to make them a habit, to incorporate certain behaviors as a *lifestyle*. By setting the example early in their lives, service to others will become a part of your children's routine as they grow (and as you grow as a family!).

"Parents hear endlessly that they are the primary religious educators of their children. This has little to do with books, memorizing the commandments or learning rules and regulations. Wise parents leave that to the second or third most important form of religious education, the kind that happens in a religious education program. Kids get the most effective religious formation in the family context, and most of it originates in situations that fire the young imagination, evoke wonder, some laughter, and a question or two....parents can cultivate a sensitivity, a kind of built-in radar for events that will, if tapped, become revelations for the holy...some of the most important times in a family's life are the times of "sacred play", times where they pause, even momentarily, to remember that there is more going on in the kitchen, the living room, the bedroom and the backyard than just what meets the eye. At such times, families know that the God of the family is thick in the air.[29]"

ENDNOTES

1. See John Westerhoff III in his definitive book *Will Our Children Have Faith?* (New York: HarperCollins, 1976) p. 91

2. From an article in the Fall 2001 issue of <u>Reform Judaism</u> entitled "Awakenings", the author Dr. Rachel Naomi Remen quotes herself from her book *Kitchen Table Wisdom: Stories That Heal* (Riverhead Books, 1996) p. 28

3. Westerhoff, *ibid.*, p.89

4. Sophia Cavaletti, *The Religious Potential of the Child* (Chicago: Liturgy Training Publication, 1992), p. 17

5. The work of V. Bailey Gillespie is utilized throughout this section, compiled from his text *The Experience of Faith* (Birmingham, Alabama: Religious Education Press, 1988) p. 90

6. Quoted by author Diane Schoemperlen in her novel *Our Lady of the Lost and Found* (New York: Penguin Books, 2001) p. 121, a delightful work wherein our story's narrator discovers "Mary" the mother of Jesus standing in the corner of her living room, wearing Nikes and a scarf over her head.

7. Rabbi Michael Sternfield's, of Chicago Sinai Congregation expanding on comments in his sermon from Kol Nidre evening services, September 2002.

8. Rabbi Howard Berman, Rabbi Emeritus of Chicago Sinai Congregation, in his comments from his sermon given on Yom Kippur morning, September 15, 1994.

9. Tom McGrath, contributing editor of U.S. Catholic, in an interview reported by the Catholic New World, August 2002 and reprinted on the internet website www.catholicnewworld.com.

10. In a private conversation with Rev. John C. Cusick, director of the Office of Young Adult Ministry, the Archdiocese of Chicago when asked to explain the role of worship in our lives.

11. See Rabbi Harold Kushner in *To Life! A Celebration of Jewish Being and Thinking* (Boston: Little Brown and Co., 1993) p. 204

12. Westerhoff, *ibid.*, p. 60

13. *Psalm 47 (The Lord the King of all Nations)* found in the Saint Joseph Edition of the *New American Bible*, p. 633

14. Reprinted from the handbook Let Us Pray, a booklet on prayer prepared by Mrs. Kay Bracco for use by the Chicago Family School Families (reprinted with permission).

15. Excerpted from the Union Prayerbook, Sinai Edition (an adaptation of the Union Prayerbook Newly Revised Edition of the Central Conference of American Rabbis, Part I) Chicago Sinai Congregation, 2000, from the prayers recited during the High Holy Days, p. 104

16. See the section on prayer in the *Catechism of the Catholic Church* (Liguori, MO: Liguori, 1994) p. 632.

17. Father John C. Cusick, writing the cover story on prayer in the Winter 2002 issue of *Chicago Style, Young Adult Ministry* (printed with cooperation of New World Publications.)

18. See Harold Kushner, *To Life!*, p. 202

19. *Ibid.*, p. 209

20. See V. Bailey Gillespie, *ibid.*, p. 98

21. See the essay written by Laura Bernstein entitled "Jewish Spirituality – Guidelines for the Still Perplexed" found in *Finding a Way: Essays on Spiritual Practice*, ed. by Lorette Zirker (Charles E. Tuttle Co.: Boston, 1996) p. 106

22. See Sofia Cavaletti's *The Religious Potential of the Child*" p.128

23. Rabbi Lawrence Kushner, *God was in this place and I, I did not know (Finding Self, Spirituality and Ultimate Meaning)*, (Jewish Lights Publishing: Woodstock, VT, 1991) p.88

24. Westerhoff, *ibid.*, p.56

25. See the *New American Bible, St. Joseph Edition* (Catholic Book Publishing: New York, 1992), p. 359.

26. Excerpted from a story told by Rabbi Michael Sternfield of Chicago Sinai Congregation during the community's observance of Kol Nidre Eve, September 2002.

27. Rabbi Steven Carr Reuben, *Raising Jewish Children in a Contemporary World* (Rocklin, Calif.: Prima Publishing, 1992), p 48. While inherently a book of raising *Jewish* children, the book is an excellent resource of how to nurture *all* children.

28. Rabbi Howard Berman, Rabbi Emeritus of Chicago Sinai Congregation comments on the nature of being a religious reform Jew, during a sermon the morning of Yom Kippur, September 15, 1994.

29. See the essay by author Mitch Finley entitled "Family Rites – Doing What Comes Naturally" in the book *Rituals for Faith Sharing, ed. by John Roberto* (Don Bosco Multimedia: New Rochelle, NY, 1992), p.65

Epilogue

And so the adult has many demanding tasks to accomplish if he wants to help the child live his relationship with God.

-Sofia Cavaletti

As I sit and write, my children are no longer young. They have grown into adolescence, with its own challenges and joys, and I as a parent have needed to adapt with new skills and (hopefully) insight.

Perhaps that is our challenge as a parent: to know that we must constantly keep growing, changing, evolving in all manner of parenting, though perhaps most subtlety in the issues of faith formation (the joke used to be that as soon as we figured something out regarding our children - they went and changed on us!) We learned how important it was to know ourselves: to develop the ability to ascertain what belongs to "us" and our journey, versus what is owned by our children. We learned that we needed to re-educate ourselves to our own religious tradition, and secondly that of our spouse: we needed the necessary language in order to have the conversation. We learned to be more precise in that language, weaving our understanding of communal religion into an expression of personal belief, which might then be expressed as a private faith. We learned when to speak of faith versus when to talk of religion and belief. We came to the understanding that the experience of our children would not replicate our own, and that was a GOOD thing. Our task was to craft a new experience for our family, and we would be better for it.

We learned that by submerging ourselves into the religious tradition of our partner, our own faith became more defined and often stronger, enhanced by a profound awareness and sensitivity to the rituals, traditions and beliefs of our spouse. We learned that we must take risks, while taking care to understand the feelings of those we love who are dismayed, disappointed and most often fearful of the choices we made.

We learned to dismiss the concerns of others, especially those who had an agenda. Who wouldn't be frightened by the insinuation and intimation of others that children of interfaith marriages will feel confused, dysfunctional, neurotic, disorientated, damaged and marginalized? I would submit that those labels are a projection of how *they* feel, rather than the reality of how things are.

We have learned that there are clergy, Catholic and Jewish, who will support and cherish us and our children; who will remain available to us in a non-judgmental way; who are open to journeying beside us. We learned there are communities, parishes and synagogue alike, who will embrace us just as we are, on our terms, without pretense or falsehood.

And so, seventeen years after the journey began, I can attest that I have no regrets. As with many aspects of family life, we have journeyed together: we have prayed together, worshipped together, served our community together. Our children seem to have an identifiable relationship with a Being (an "ultimate concern" as author Paul Tillich would have it) they call God. It seems to be defined, at least on the surface, by trust, obedience and love. They also present themselves as "Catholic Jewish" as if it were a seamless garment, and never for a moment were they confused.

Our journey began with the experience of Baptism and Baby Naming. That experience touched and moved us in ways we could not have foretold. Seeing as it took us some time to come to that moment fully prepared, we took our commitment very seriously; it became our mission to accept the responsibility of the promises we made then. For those who now come to that place, I wish you well, knowing that you are not alone and that the hand of God and the mystery of His unconditional grace will guide you on your way.

Amen.

Appendix

In gratitude and love, I would like to mention the following artists and their contributions to this work:

Page 10	*Green Cross,* by Travis W., age 6
Page 14	*Advent Calendar,* by Emily Z., age 11
Page 18	*Jesus,* by Eliza R., age 9
Page 28	*Trees, Flowers, Sun & Rainbow on earth, by Nate J., age 10*
Page 43	*Church,* by Kate D., age 10
Page 47	*Wheel,* by Ben S., age 13 (with the help of his computer!)
Page 50	*Dove (Jesus),* by Tim S., age 9
Page 54	*The Two Faces of God,* by Hannah R., age 9
Page 57	*Communion Wafer,* by Nora S., age 11
Page 58	*Dancing Jesus,* by Sophie R., age 8
Page 60	*The Globe,* by Ben S., age 10
Page 63	*God,* by Eliza R., age 9
Page 65	*Jesus Christ,* by Sophia U., age 11
Page 68	*Jewish Star,* by Ben S., age 13
Page 69	*The Parting of the Red Sea,* by Hannah R., age 9
Page 70	*Jesus (Girl by the fire),* by Emily Z., age 9
Page 76	*Noah's Ark,* by Mikey S., age 5
Page 91	*Interfaith Mosaic* by Nica J., age 8
Page 93	*God,* by Marie Claude R., age 8
Page 94	*Jesus,* by Kate D., age 8
Page 96	*Crucifixion,* by Sydney S., age 10
Page 100	*Cross,* by Ben S., age 13
Page 101	*Menorah,* by Emily Z., age 9
Page 127	*Stained Glass Windows and Pews,* by Ethan L., age 6
Page 133	*Shabbat Shalom (Sh'ma and Jewish Boy),* by Willie K., age 8
Page 139	*Jesus,* by Molly G., age 9
Page 144	*Christmas Tree,* by Emily Z., age 9
Page 147	*Sh'ma,* by Nora S., age 11
Page 149	*Sukkah,* by Emily Z., age 11
Page 161	*God,* by Maya R., age 10

Resources

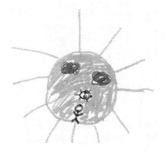

Over the past several years, a number of resources, printed and otherwise, have entered the marketplace concerned with issues confronting interfaith families: their lives and those of their children; their prayers; their rituals. Below you will find a listing of those books and internet addresses, compiled according to topic area and interest.

ADULT LEARNING/FAITH FORMATION

Abrams, Elliot. *Faith or Fear*. New York: The Free Press, 1997

Berman, Louis. *Jews and Intermarriage: A Study in Personality and Culture*. New York: Tomas Yoseloff, 1968

Borg, Marcus. *Meeting Jesus Again for the First Time*. San Francisco: Harper Books, 1994

Boys, Mary C. *Has God Only One Blessing? Judaism as Source of Christian Self-Understanding*. New York: Stimulas Book, 2000

Brown, Rev. Raymond. *An Introduction to the New Testament*. New York: Doubleday, 1997

Cahill, Thomas. *The Gift of the Jews: How a Tribe of Desert Nomads Changed the Way Everyone Thinks and Feels*. New York: Doubleday, 1998

Carroll, James. *Constantine's Sword…The Church and the Jews*. New York: Houghton Mifflin, 2001

Catalano, Rosann; Sandmel, David and Christopher Leighton, editors. *Irreconcilable Differences? A Learning Resource for Jews and Christians*. Westview Press, 2001

Cavaletti, Sophia. *The Religious Potential of the Child*. Ramsey, New Jersey: Paulist Press, 1983

Coles, Dr. Robert. *The Spiritual Lives of Children*. Boston: Houghton Mifflin., 1990

Crossan, John Dominic. *The Birth of Christianity: Discovering What Happened in the Years Immediately After the Execution of Jesus*. San Francisco: HarperCollins, 1998

Donin, Rabbi Hayim Halevy. *To Be A Jew: A Guide to Jewish Observance in Contemporary Life*. New York: Basic Books, 1972

Fowler, James W. and Sam Keen. *Life Maps: Conversations on the Journey of Faith*. Waco, Texas: Word   Books, 1978

Glaser, Gabrielle. *Strangers To The Tribe, Portraits of Interfaith Marriage*. Boston: Houghton Mifflin Co., 1997

Gillespie, V. Bailey. *The Experience of Faith*. Birmingham: Religious Education Press, 1988

Goldman, Ari L. *Being Jewish: The Spiritual and Cultural Practice of Judaism Today*. New York: Simon and Schuster, 2000

Johnson, Luke Timothy. *The Real Jesus: The Misguided Quest for the Historical Jesus and the Truth of the Traditional Gospels*. San Francisco: HarperCollins, 1996

Kushner, Rabbi Harold. *Who Needs God?* New York: Summit, 1989

----- *To Life! A Celebration of Jewish Being and Thinking*. Boston: Warner Books, 1993

Kushner, Lawrence. *God Was in this Place and I, I Did Not Know*. Jewish Lights Publishing, 1991

------*Jewish Spirituality, A Brief Introduction for Christians*. Jewish Lights Publishing, 2001

Lewis, C.S.. *Mere Christianity*. San Francisco: HarperCollins, 1952

Matthews, Gareth. *The Philosophy of Childhood*. Cambridge, Mass: Harvard University Press, 1994

Mayer, Dr. Egon. *Children of Intermarriage: A Study in Patterns of Identification and Jewish Life*. New York: The American Jewish Committee, 1983

------*Love and Tradition: Marriage Between Christians and Jews*. New York: Plenum Press, 1985

Norris, Kathleen. *Amazing Grace, a Vocabulary of Faith*. New York: Riverhead Books, 1998

Panati, Charles. *Sacred Origins of Profound Things*. New York: Penguin Books, 1996

Roiphe, Anne. *Generation Without Memory: A Jewish Journey in Christian America*. New York: The Linden Press/Simon and Schuster, 1981

Rosenbaum, Mary Helene & Ned. *Celebrating Our Differences*. Shippensberg, PA: Ragged Edge Press, 1994

Rosenberg, Rabbi Roy A., Rev. Peter Meehan and Rev. John Wade Payne. *Happily Intermarried: Authoritative Advice for A Joyous Jewish-Christian Marriage*. New York: Macmillan, 1988

Schneider, Susan Weidman. *Intermarriage: The Challenge of Living with Differences Between Christians and Jews*. New York: The Free Press, 1989

Schulweis, Harold M. *Finding Each Other in Judaism: Meditations on the Rites of Passage from Birth to Immortality*. New York: UAHC Press, 2001

Silverstein, Alan. *It All Begins With a Date*. Northvale, NJ: Jason Aronson, inc., 1995

Spoto, Donald. *The Hidden Jesus: a New Life*. New York: St. Martin's Press, 1998

Rizzuto, Ana-Maria. *The Birth of the Living God*. Chicago: University of Chicago Press, 1979

Teluskin, Rabbi Joseph. *Biblical Literacy*. New York: William Morrow & Co., 1997

Waskow, Arthur. *Down-To-Earth Judaism: Food, Money, Sex and the Rest of Life*. New York: William Morrow & Co., 1995

Westerhoff, Rev. John. *Will Our Children Have Faith?*, New York: Seabury Press, 1976.

Wilkes, Paul. *The Good Enough Catholic—A Guide for the Perplexed.* New York: Ballatine Books, 1996.

FAMILY LEARNING

Berends, Polly Berrien. *Gently Lead – How to Teach Your Children About God.* New York: HarperCollins, 1992

Bernardin, Joseph Cardinal and Catholic Jewish Dialogue. *A Blessing to Each Other.* Chicago: Liturgy Training Publications, 1996

Bennett, William J., editor. *The Moral Compass.* New York: Simon & Schuster, 1995

-----*The Book of Virtues.* New York: Simon & Schuster, 1993

Coffey, Kathy. *Experiencing God with Your Children.* New York: Crossroad Publishing, 1998

Cowan, Paul with Rachel Cowan. *Mixed Blessings: Marriage Between Christians and Jews.* New York: Doubleday, 1987

Crohn, Dr. Joel. *Mixed Matches: How To Create Successful Interracial, Interethnic and Interfaith Relationships.* New York: Fawcett Columbine, 1995

Diamant, Anita with Karen Kushner. *How to Be a Jewish Parent: A Practical Handbook for Family Life.* New York: Schocken Books, 2000

Dosick, Wayne. *Golden Rules-The Ten Ethical Values Parents Need to Teach Their Children.* San Francisco: HarperCollins, 1995

Eyre, Linda and Richard. *Teaching Your Children Values.* New York: Fireside, 1993

Fay, Martha. *Do Children Need Religion? How Parents Today are Thinking about the Big Questions.* New York: Pantheon, 1993

Fishman, Sylvia Barack. *Jewish and Something Else: A Study of Mixed Married Families.* NY: AJC, 2001

Fitzpatrick, Jean Grasso. *Once Upon a Family –Read Aloud Stories and Activities that Nurture Healthy Kids.* New York: Viking, 1998

-----*Small Wonder-How To Answer Your Child's Impossible Questions About Life.* New York: Viking, 1994

-----*Something More-Nurturing Your Child's Spiritual Growth.* New York: Viking, 1991

Friedland, Ronnie and Edmund Case, editors. *The Guide to Jewish Interfaith Family Life: An InterfaithFamily.com Handbook.* Woodstock, VT: Jewish Lights Publishing, 2001

Freedman, Rabbi E.B., Jan Greenberg and Karen Katz. *What does being Jewish Mean? Read Aloud Responses to Questions Jewish Children ask about History, Religion and Culture.* New York: Fireside Books, 1991

Gellman, Rabbi Marc and Monsignor Thomas Hartman. *Where Does God Live?* New York: Ballantine Books, 1991

Goodman-Malamuth Leslie and Robin Margolis. *Between Two worlds: Choices for Grown Children of Jewish-Christian Parents.* New York: Pocket Books, 1992

Gruzen, Lee F. *Raising Your Jewish/Christian Child: How Interfaith Parents Can Give Their Children the Best of Both Their Heritages.* New York: Newmarket Press, 1990

Heller, Dr. David. *Talking To Your Children About God.* New York: Perigee Books, 1988

Hollander, Annette, M.D. *How To Help Your Child Have A Spiritual Life: A Parent's Guide To Inner Development.* New York: A&W Publishers, Inc., 1980

Jacobs, Rabbi Sidney J. and Betty J. *122 Clues for Jews Whose Children Intermarry.* Culver City, CA: Jacobs Ladder Publications, 1988

Kilpatrick, William, & Gregory and Suzanne Wolfe. *Books that Build Character.* New York: Touchstone, 1994

King, Andrea. *If I'm Jewish and You're Catholic, What are the Kids?* New York: UAHC Press, 1993

Levin, Sunie. *Mingled Roots: A Guide for Jewish Grandparents of Interfaith Grandchildren.* New York: B'nai B'rith Women, 1991

Nolte, Dorothy Law, & Rachel Harris. *Children Learn What they Live-Parenting to Inspire Values.* New York: Workman Publishing, 1998

Petsonk, Judy & Jim Remsen. *The Intermarriage Handbook: A Guide for Christians and Jews.* New York: Arbor House/William Morrow & Co., 1988

Reed, Bobbie. *501 Practical Ways to Teach Your Children Values.* St. Louis: Concordia Publishing House, 1998

Reuben, Rabbi Steven Carr. *But How Will You Raise the Children? A Guide to Interfaith Marriage.* New York: Pocket Books, 1987

Wolpe, Rabbi David. *Teaching Your Children About God.* New York: Henry Holt & Co., 1993

Yount, Christine, editor. *Helping Children Know God---140 Practical Ideas to Help Your Children Grow in Faith.* Loveland, CO: Group Books, 1995

Yribarren, Denise & DeAnn Koestner. *Make Family Time Prime Time Fun---Fun Ways to Build Faith in Your Family.* Mystic, CT: Twenty-Third Publications, 1997

CELEBRATING RITUALS AND PRAYER

On the Doorposts of Your House: Prayers and Ceremonies for the Jewish Home. New York: CCAR Press, 1994

The Oxford Book of Prayer. New York: Oxford University press, 1985

Imber-Black, Evan and Janine Roberts. *Rituals for Our Times: Celebrating, Healing and Changing Our Lives and Our Relationships.* New York: HarperCollins, 1992

Berg, Elizabeth. *Family Traditions—Celebrations for Holidays and Everyday.* Pleasantville, NY: Reader's Digest, 1992

Cox, Harvey. *Common Prayers: Faith Family and a Christian's Journey through the Jewish Year*. New York: Houghton Mifflin, 2001

Edwards, Michelle. *Blessed Are You, Traditional Hebrew Prayers*. New York: Lothrop, Lee & Shepard Books, 1993

Farry, Ginger. *Through Family Times: A Conversational Prayerbook for Today's World*. Mahway, NJ: Paulist Press, 1993

Groner, Judyth and Madeline Wikler. *Thank You God! A Jewish Child's Book of Prayers*. Rockville, MD: Kar-Ben Copies, Inc., 1993

Haas, David. *Dear God...Prayers for Children*. New York: Crossroad Publishing, 1997

Mayer, Nan. *The Interfaith Family Seder Book: How to Celebrate a Jewish Passover Supper with Christian In-Laws and Non-Jewish Friends*. New York: Heritage, 1998

Nelson, Gertrude Mueller. *To Dance with God---Family Ritual and Community Celebration*. New York: Paulist Press, 1986

----- *Child of God-A Book of Birthdays and Days in Between*. Chicago: Liturgy Training Publications, 1997

Roberts, Elizabeth and Elias Amidon, editors. *Earth Prayers From Around the World*. San Francisco: HarperCollins, 1991

BOOKS FOR KIDS

FOR WEE LITTLE ONES...

Allen, Nicholas. *Jesus' Christmas Party*. New York: Doubleday, 2001

Conan, Sally Anne. *Thank You God*. Mahweh, NJ: Paulist Press, 1997

----*Look and See What God Gave Me*. Mahweh, NJ: Paulist Press, 1997

----*God's Best Gift*. Mahweh, NJ: Paulist Press, 1997

Drucker, Malka. *Grandma's Latkes*. New York: The Trumpet Club, 1992

Griffin, William. *Jesus for Children.* Mystic, CN: Twenty-Third Publications, 1994

Hawxhurst, Joan C. *Bubbe & Gram: My Two Grandmothers.* Kalamazoo, MI: Dovetail Publishing, 1997

Kushner, Lawrence and Karen Kushner. *Because Nothing Looks Like God.* Skylight Paths, 2001

Lewis, Shari & Florence Henderson. *One Minute Bible Stories: The Old Testament.* New York: Dell, 1986

----- *One Minute Bible Stories: The New Testament.* New York: Dell, 1986

McDermott, Gerald. *Raven, A Trickster Tale from the Pacific Northwest.* San Francisco: Harcourt Brace & Co., 1993

Moorman, Margaret. *Light the Lights, A Story Celebrating Hanukkah and Christmas.* New York: Cartwheel Books, 1994

Okrend, Elise and Philip. *Blintzes for Blitzen.* 1996

Sasso, Rabbi Sandy Eisenberg. *In God's Name.* Vermont: Jewish Lights Publishing, 1994

-----*A Prayer for the Earth: The Story of Naamah, Noah's Wife.* Vermont: Jewish Lights Publishing, 2001

Schotter, Roni. *Hanukkah!* New York: The Trumpet Club, 1990

Spier, Peter. *Noah's Ark.* New York: Dell, 1992

Swartz, Nancy Sohn. *In Our Image: God's First Creatures.* Vermont: Jewish Lights Publishing, 2000

FOR MIDDLE READERS...

Bunting, Eve. *Terrible Things, An Allegory of the Holocaust.* New York: Harper & Row, 1980

DePaola, Tomie. *The Night of the Posadas.* Putnam, 2001

Freedland, Sara. *Hanukkah!* Candlewick Press, 2001

Gertz, Susan Enid. *Hanukkah and Christmas at My House.* Willow and Laurel Press, 1992

Godden, Rumer. *Prayers from the Ark.* New York: Viking, 1992

Green, Donna. *Christmas at Our House (a workbook).* New York: Smithmark, 1995

Hoffman, Mary. *Three Wise Women.* Penguin Putnam, 2001

L'Engle, Madeleine. *Ladder of Angels, Stories of the Bible.* New York: Harper & Row, 1979

Rosen, Michael. *Elijah's Angel.* San Francisco: Harcourt Brace, 1992

Schwartz, Cherie Karo. *My Lucky Dreidel (Hanukkah Stories, Songs, Poems, Crafts, Recipes and Fun for Kids).* New York: Smithmark, 1994

FOR OLDER READERS...

Blume, Judy. *Are You There God? It's Me, Margaret.* New York: Yearling Book, 1970

Goodrich Frances and Albert Hackett. *The Diary of Anne Frank* (published as a dramatic play). New York: Random House, 1956

Patterson, Katherine. *The Preacher's Boy.* New York: Clarion Books, 1999

Singer, Issac Bashevis. *Stories for Children.* New York: Farrar/Straus/Giroux, 1995

----- *The Power of Light.* New York: Sunburst Books, 1980

Wangerin, Walter Jr. *Potter.* Augsburg Publications, 1994

RESOURCES ON THE WORLD WIDE WEB

www.beliefnet.com - An excellent resource on a variety of religious traditions, from Baha'i to Zoroastrianism. The site offers reflections on Family and Life Events, Health and Healing, News and Society, Morality, Relationships, Teens and more, always with the underpinnings of religious belief.

www.clickonjudaism.org - This site is a project of the Reform Movement's Union of American Hebrew Congregations Commission on Outreach and Synagogue Community. The purpose of the site, according to the author, is "to provide doorways into Judaism for Jews in their 20's and 30's." This site does have a good bibliography, as well as recent articles on a variety of subjects of interest to those intermarried.

www.crosscurrents.org- A magazine dealing with "connecting the wisdom of the heart and life of the mind, bringing people together across lines of difference."

www.conexuspress.com - "The mission of CoNexus Press includes providing opportunities for individuals to make connections with interfaith and service organizations." This site has a broad inventory of links to other religious websites.

www.dovetailinstitute.org - The Dovetail Institute for Interfaith Family Resources is a "not-for-profit organization not affiliated with any religious denomination. Respecting the right and need of Jewish and Christian partners to explore the spiritual and religious dimensions of an interfaith household", this site offers a link to their educational and networking capabilities. Also provides a link to their journal.

www.interfaithcommunity.org - The site of the Jewish Christian community in the New York metropolitan area.

www.interfaithfamily.com This is an on-line publication which is issued monthly, regarding Jewish intermarried family and life. While decidedly Jewish in content, there is always an articulate Christian sentiment.

www.jcrelations.net - A site devoted to the work, insights and issues in the on-going Jewish Christian Dialogue of an international council, with 37 member organizations from 32 countries. This site is an excellent resource for other links to learning.

www.joi.org - This site reflects the efforts of a national organization, dedicated to community-based outreach. This site offers a broad library of learning, statewide guide to Outreach programs, news and events and a vast holiday section on Jewish celebrations.

www.judaism.about.com - A site with excellent references to Hebrew baby names.

www.mixedblessing.com - A store of holiday greeting cards and products for interfaith families.

www.myjewishlearning.com - A new site created in November 2002 and underwritten by the Bronfman Endowment in conjunction with Hebrew College, this site is a vast education resource on a variety of topics concerned with Jewish life, culture, history and Bible.

www.newadvent.org - A Catholic encyclopedia, listed by alphabet; also a variety of helpful links for issues relating to Catholic doctrine and theology.

www.patpapers.com - The source for interfaith greeting cards, home of "Just Mishpucha" and "Mishpucha Et al.

www.ritualr.com/hebrewnames.htm The site is "Ritual Reality", but an excellent resource for Jewish baby names and their meaning.

www.smartmarriages.com - The source for current research on how to make your marriage 'smarter', happier and more satisfying.

www.uahc.org/outreach - The homepage for the UAHC, with a link to their outreach department.

Printed in the United States
81059LV00003B/232-234